5
LEADERSHIP
ESSENTIALS
for Women

OTHER NEW HOPE BOOKS BY

Linda Clark

*Awaken the Leader in You: 10 Life Essentials
for Women in Leadership*

*Found Treasures: Discovering Your Worth in
Unexpected Places*

REVISED AND UPDATED

5 LEADERSHIP ESSENTIALS for Women

Developing Your Ability to Make Things Happen

COMPILED BY LINDA CLARK

NEW HOPE® PUBLISHERS
Gospel-Centered. Missions-Driven.

BIRMINGHAM, ALABAMA

New Hope® Publishers
P. O. Box 12065
Birmingham, AL 35202-2065
NewHopeDigital.com

Library of Congress Cataloging-in-Publication Data
    5 leadership essentials for women : developing your ability to make things happen / compiled by Linda Clark.
        pages cm
    ISBN 978-1-59669-431-6 (sc)
    1. Christian leadership. 2. Women in church work. I. Clark, Linda, 1944- compiler. II. Title: Five leadership essentials for women.
    BV652.1.A12 2015
    248.8′43--dc23
                            2014045735

Scripture quotations marked (NIV) are taken from the Holy Bible, New International Version®, NIV®. Copyright © 1973, 1978, 1984, 2011 by Biblica, Inc.™ Used by permission of Zondervan. All rights reserved worldwide. www.zondervan.com The "NIV" and "New International Version" are trademarks registered in the United States Patent and Trademark Office by Biblica, Inc.™

Scripture quotations marked (KJV) are taken from The Holy Bible, King James Version.

Scripture quotations marked (NKJV) are taken from the New King James Version. Copyright © 1982 by Thomas Nelson, Inc. Used by permission. All rights reserved.

Scripture quotations marked (Phillips) are taken from THE NEW TESTAMENT IN MODERN ENGLISH, Revised Edition, J.B. Phillips, translator. © J.B. Phillips 1958, 1960, 1972. By permission of Macmillan Publishing Co., Inc.

Scripture quotations marked (TLB) are taken from *The Living Bible*, copyright© 1971. Used by permission of Tyndale House Publishers, Inc., Wheaton, IL. All rights reserved.

Interior Design: Glynese Northam

ISBN-10: 1-59669-431-9
ISBN-13: 978-59669-431-6

N154110 • 0515 • 2M1

CONTENTS

INTRODUCTION

By Linda Clark

And the peace of God, which transcends all understanding, will guard your hearts and your minds in Christ Jesus. Finally, brothers and sisters, whatever is true, whatever is noble, whatever is right, whatever is pure, whatever is lovely, whatever is admirable — if anything is excellent or praiseworthy — think about such things.

— PHILIPPIANS 4:7–8

True leaders form as they face challenges and difficult times when results seem negligible or nonexistent. It is then that a woman's heart and mind are tested. The leadership position she holds may not be one she sought, or it may be one she volunteered to do because of her passion for the cause. Her expertise may put her into a thankless situation, one in which her persistence, loyalty, and abilities are thrown into a blazing-hot fiery furnace!

During times like these, women in leadership positions must pause and answer some hard questions. *Why am I doing this? Can I be an influence for good? Do I have the necessary skills to do the job? Is God directing my steps?*

When we as female leaders feel overwhelmed, we must not only have the skills to navigate leadership storms but also believe that what we are doing will make a difference in others' lives, have an impact on a movement or cause, and equip others to assume leadership roles of their own. Assessing our skills is a huge part of what leaders must do to stay ahead of inevitable *change*.

When I was first asked to write a compilation for a leadership skills book, I was committed to a project that would help women improve their leadership skill sets. I am honored that ten years later I have been asked to revise and update that book. A book on leadership *for* women *by* women is a good thing! This revision will readdress the five critical elements of a woman's leadership abilities: communication, relationships, time management, conflict management, and group building.

5 Leadership Essentials brings these topics to your attention again so that as you face new, challenging situations in leadership, you will be aware. None of these five areas of concern has remained the same since 2004. If you have been in any leadership capacity during that time, you can attest to that!

- Because technological advances continue, we need to rethink the chapter on communication.
- The way people look at their relationships has drastically morphed into things we might never have expected. We need to reassess our approach to the relationships we have as leaders.
- While each of us still has only 24 hours a day, the demands on that time may have dramatically changed. Many women still work an eight-hour day outside the home while others are as productive while working mostly or exclusively within

their homes. Work-for-pay may look a lot different to you than it did several years ago. Lines between the workplace and home life have blurred, at times making it impossible to see where one begins and the other ends. There are other changes women face.

- At work and at home, there is no shortage of conflict. I hope some new thoughts about conflict management will sharpen your ability to deal with it as it arises.
- And then, there are those pesky issues that can arise in many groups! If the members of a group you are struggling to lead would, you think, *Pay attention and get on my page, I could get something done.* This *5 Leadership Essentials* revision can change your thinking and give you fresh viewpoints.

We as women have never shied away from taking on leadership roles. How effective we are and how we grow as leaders might be other matters. As we follow God's leading out of our comfort zones, launch new ministries, develop new skills, and more, we can rest in God's promise that He "will guard [our] hearts and [our] minds in Christ Jesus" (Philippians 4:7).

It is my hope that this book content will lead you to discover new insights, gain fresh perspectives, and renew your leadership spirit. My prayer is that you will allow God to speak to your specific leadership needs through this new and improved *5 Leadership Essentials!*

In His Service,

Linda M. Clark

Note: If you wish to contact me, please connect with me by email: lclark1213@hotmail.com

SPOTLIGHT ON WOMEN

Here are some statistics that might catch your attention:
- In 2020, 156 women for every 100 men will earn college degrees.
- 48% of women participate in community or civic groups or causes.
- 74% of women say that lack of time is a major issue for them.
- 63% of women indicate they have a lack of energy to do the things they need to do.

How do these statements influence women in the workplace?
- Women tend to be more inclusive in positions of leadership.
- Women show little interest in titles or perks in the workplace.
- Women generally lead from the center, rather than from the top.
- Women prefer direct communication and want information to come directly from the source.

Are women more effective as leaders than men? Many past stereotypes are incorrect. Look at the following statistics from a recent survey.
- Women rank higher in taking initiative and are more results-oriented.
- Women demonstrat more interest in developing others as leaders.
- Women favor change more than men.
- Women score higher in building relationships and inspiring others.
- The survey indicated women appear stronger at getting things done, in being role models, and delivering results.

Source: Zenger Foundation, 2014.

WHAT RESOURCES SAY ABOUT TODAY'S WOMEN

Want to find out more about how women function in the workplace, build relationships, manage their time and conflict, or build groups? These groups' websites may be of interest to you:
- Digital Marketing Sources
- Time Inc. Women's Group
- Pew Internet and American Life
- Faith Popcorn's Brain Reserve
- Parenting Group
- Real Simple magazine studies

1 COMMUNICATION ESSENTIALS

By Harriet Harral

*"It has been said that the meaning of communica-
tion is in the response it gets."*

— CAROL FLEMING, speech pathologist

Every leader must spend some time considering how she
communicates. We communicate all the time! Isn't that
a scary thought? What messages am I sending to my listeners
or readers? What will you retain? What will you forget even
as you turn the page? The answers to these questions are as
varied as the readers. That is why the study of communication
is so complex, so rewarding, so frustrating, so much fun, so
immediate, and so far-reaching.

This chapter will not answer all of your questions, or make
you an expert communicator. My prayer is that it will give you
some new ideas and perhaps cause you to think anew about
some old ones. I hope it will alert you to some pitfalls and
some opportunities. My goal is to help you improve how you
communicate, to point out patterns, assist your planning as a
leader, and open windows of understanding between you and
those with whom you work.

In this section you will become better acquainted with some women in leadership roles, whose stories are told in the Old and New Testaments. Each part of the chapter will deal with one particular communication skill needed by a leader. Learning a new skill involves seeing it modeled, having it explained, trying it ourselves, practicing the skill, and then evaluating how we are doing.

I hope that the following discussions about communication will help you to become a more confident leader. As you read, keep in mind that an effective communicator always focuses on the person listening. Our focus should always be to lead in such a way that *others* will see Christ in us.

~ SAY WHAT? HOW WE COMMUNICATE ~

Abigail, an intelligent woman, was the wife of Nabal, a wealthy man who was surly and mean. David and his men arrived in Nabal's territory during the festive time of sheep shearing and approached Nabal with greetings, asking for food. Afraid his servants would leave if he gave away resources, Nabal scornfully refused David and his men and sent them away. David was furious and swore he would kill every male in the household of Nabal.

One of Abigail's servants ran to warn her of the danger from David and explained that David's people had been very kind to them. Abigail immediately gathered donkey-loads of bread, wine, fruit, and grain. Without telling Nabal, she and her servants traveled to David's camp.

As soon as Abigail saw David, she fell to the ground and apologized for her husband's actions. She then acknowledged David's destiny as king and predicted a great future for him. She argued that in his time of success, David would not want the staggering burden of needless bloodshed on his conscience.

Persuaded by Abigail, David thanked her for saving him from the burden of vengefulness. Abigail went home and told Nabal what she had done. His heart failed, and he soon died. When David heard of this, he sent for Abigail to become his wife (this story is based on 1 Samuel 25).

Abigail was an excellent communicator. She models for us the most effective approach we can take to understand and be understood. Isn't that what communication is all about? It certainly is what this chapter is about!

COMMUNICATION CHOICES

What is your reaction to the following statements? Think for a moment about the communication process.

- ☒ Communication influences your relationships.
- ☒ How you communicate affects your ability to be a good leader.
- ☒ Ethical communication demonstrates respect and concern for all involved.
- ☒ True communication requires that we accept others' freedom of choice.
- ☒ Our attitudes toward others in communication are more significant than the content of the message.
- ☒ Making choices is a part of the communication process.
- ☒ Technology has dramatically altered how we communicate.
- ☒ Technology can undermine effective communication.

Regardless of how you responded to these statements, the fact is, communication is a series of choices we make. We choose whether to speak. We choose how to say what we want to say. We choose whether to laugh, cry over, or applaud responses to what we say. Sometimes all the options are desirable, and we want them all. Sometimes the options seem undesirable, and we want to avoid all of them. See, even that's a choice!

STRINGS AND CANS

Did you ever make your own telephone using two soup cans and a long string? Children used to love to make these communication devices and pretend they were one another. I suspect that now, they use their own cell phones or borrow their parents' mobiles! I recently saw an illustration of communication that I especially liked: tangled wires in-between two people. It is truly a miracle if what we say is interpreted correctly and results in clarifying any situation. The tangled mess between the sender and the receiver represents what we say, what the listener thinks we said, what we really meant, and what action results from what we've said.

There are three steps in any communication that takes place. First are the sender's *thoughts*. It can be an idea or instruction for action. Second, *encoding* takes place. This step is the actual message in words or other symbols. The third step, *decoding*, occurs when the receiver translates the message into something she or he can understand.

It is not difficult to see how easily communication can derail during any one of these three steps. When we communicate, we want the receiver to form a picture in her or his mind that is exactly like the one in ours. We want change to take place, understanding to happen, and action to occur as a result of what we have said. Of course, not all communication is verbal. Other communication options will be discussed later in this chapter.

While you are still thinking about how effective your attempts to communicate are ...

TRY THIS

- Take a piece of paper, close your eyes, and write your name and address at the top of the page. Draw a map showing where your house is located. Make notes on the map of any points of reference that would be helpful. Now look at what you've drawn.
- How accurate is your drawing? If you had someone guiding your drawing, would it be more accurate? Having the active participation of a receiver would have helped. This is true of all communication.

MORE ABOUT THE COMMUNICATION PROCESS

Communication is a *process*. Instead of trying to delineate a specific cause or beginning, communication is continuous. Our choices are influenced by elements of our past and present of which we may be unaware. Any communication choice we make does not end once it is completed. It may have ramifications as communication continues. We learn more about ourselves and others and continue to change with them as our communication continues.

Communication is a *gestalt* — a totality depending on all our systems.

> *Webster's Dictionary* defines **gestalt**: *"A structure, configuration, or pattern of physical, biological, or*

*psychological phenomena so integrated as to consti-
tute a functional unit with properties not derivable
by summation of its parts."*

Our internal systems (attitudes, emotions, understandings,
background, psychological well-being, physical health, and so
on) interface with our external systems (situation, time, place,
urgency, ritual, and so on) to provide an opportunity to gain
understanding. Each new communication situation is unique.
Because of what we have learned about ourselves and others
in the interim, we view similar situations differently each time
we are in them.

Communication is *perceptual, creative.* No two people receive the same message in exactly the same way. Our
frames of reference are necessarily different because of the
differences in our backgrounds, information, interests, attitudes, and so on. To the extent that our experiences are similar, we may tend to interpret events similarly. To the extent we
differ, our interpretations probably differ.

Communication is *uncertain.* We can never predict
exactly what will happen in a communication situation, can
we? Human beings do not provide exact responses to particular stimuli; we are unpredictable.

❧ HOW DID ABIGAIL COMMUNICATE? ❧

*Abigail was a transactional communicator. She understood that
this communication took place in an ongoing process of communication and could only be assessed in light of the relationship
between David, Nabal, and their servants. She looked at the
entire situation, its totality, and realized the inappropriateness*

*of Nabal's response in light of David's expectations. She imme-
diately tried to understand the message Nabal had sent from
the point of view of David's men and knew that the perception
David and his men would have of Nabal would be extremely
negative. She considered Nabal's state of mind and knew that
it was not the time to try to reason with him. Uncertain as to
the outcome, she was willing to risk that, in a transaction with
David, she could prevail on his values and attitudes in such a
way that he would eventually agree with her.*

LEADERS AND COMMUNICATION

When we behave as if all communication begins and ends with
us, we are in for some troubling times! If we give the impression
that our opinion is the only one that matters, our groups will
feel significant. It certainly means they won't feel motivated to
participate. On the other hand, consider how you feel when
your opinions are sought out, when someone listens to you
and maybe even changes their mind, when you truly feel that
you are connected and involved with another person. These
should be our goals as effective leaders and communicators.

HEAR THIS

The ethics of communication have to do with our attitudes
toward others in any relationship. Those attitudes determine the kind of relationship — and the kind of communication — we will have. Accepting others and their range of
choices and accepting our own choices is a challenge for us as
leaders as we demonstrate ethical communication.

One of the greatest challenges leaders have today is related
to the technological advances that have taken place. There is

virtually no area of life left untouched by these changes! If you'd like to have an etiquette guideline to technological communicating, Phyllis Mindell's *How to Say It for Women* is a good resource. There is a *right* way and a *wrong* way to use technology in your communication.

More about this later in the chapter. First, let's look at perception and how it influences how we communicate, whether we are the sender or the receiver.

DID YOU SAY WHAT I HEARD?

Why do two people have great difficulty in communicating while two others seem to see the world the same way? Our communication rests on our perceptions of each other and of the world around us. We know that perception is a personal, individual process drawing on our experiences, attitudes, background, and values. All people see the world from their own vantage point.

Think of the implications these widely differing perceptions have on communication. Sometimes I think it is one of God's great miracles that we can ever understand another person at all!

It will help to have a basic understanding of how the process of perception works. Knowing its structure may help you identify a point at which your perception and that of another person may differ. It may also give you a way to avoid some misunderstandings or to clear up some misperceptions.

When we perceive something, at least four processes are occurring almost simultaneously. Each of the four is followed by an activity you can do to help you further understand how important perception is to the communication process. We are never able to perceive all of any event. It is overwhelming to try to perceive all that is happening around us. There will always be aspects of which we are simply unaware. Let's look at each of them.

The first step in the perception process is selectivity.

How do we select what we perceive? Several factors influence our selection. For instance, there are *physiological* factors that have an impact on our perception. Sometimes we cannot see or hear something clearly. Hearing only parts of a conversation, being seated behind a post, or hearing a wreck at the other end of the block are examples where your perception was limited because of physiological factors.

There are also *psychological* factors that influence what we select to perceive. We pay attention to things that interest us. For instance, if you are driving down the street when you are very hungry, you will probably notice the fast food advertisements. You are interested in anything that says food! We often see what we are interested in seeing. If we want harmony, we will see it. If we are looking for a fight, we will see only those elements that justify the fight.

The third factor influencing how we select what to perceive is *past experience and learning.* Have you ever been in the midst of trying to solve a problem when someone else, maybe unfamiliar with what you were doing, looked at your work, and said, "Why don't you try it this way?" and you suddenly realized they were right? Sometimes we are so familiar with something, so sure we know how something works, that we are unable to find the creative answer that solves our problem.

Keep in mind that selectivity is not bad. Of course, it can also be the reason for inefficiency, missing important indicators, or completely different understandings of a situation.

TRY THIS

Sit quietly for a moment. Try to identify everything that is happening in your environment.

1. What are the sounds you hear?
2. What do you see?
3. Have you considered everything in all directions?
4. What do you feel? (Consider physical sensations and emotional ones.)
5. What are the smells around you?

Now, considering any other people in your immediate area, what is each one of them doing, seeing, hearing, feeling, smelling, and so on?

Another part of perception is expectation.

Once we have selected those aspects of a situation to which we are going to pay attention, the next step in perception is that we begin to make some predictions, or base some expectations on those things we selected. This process is how we stereotype people. Stereotypes are no more than predictions about people based on a few, selected characteristics. Expectations are not bad, but we have to be careful not to get locked into a specific set of expectations. It means that we need to always remember that our perceptions are selective; we never have the whole picture. I saw this slogan on the sign outside a church recently: "Beware of half-truths. You may have the wrong half." We can use the process of expectation in positive ways as well as negative ones. Expectations can become self-fulfilling prophecies. If we expect the very best of ourselves and others, we often get it!

TRY THIS

In the space beside each word listed below, put the first thing that comes to your mind as an expectation about people with that characteristic.

- Blonde-haired persons: _____
- Doctors: _____
- Musicians: _____
- Athletes: _____
- Missionaries: _____
- Preachers' kids: _____
- Women CEOs: _____

Now go back and think of an exception to each of the expectations you listed.

A third part of perception: emotional reactions

It is impossible to avoid some sort of emotional reaction to any situation we perceive. Some of our reactions are obviously a lot stronger than others. In any case, our emotions influence the totality of our reaction. Sometimes I agree with you because I like you. Sometimes I like you because I agree with you!

When our emotions are particularly strong, we need to be careful that we are not overcome by them. It is hard to love someone when they are doing something that makes us very angry. However, that is what we are commanded to do in the

Bible. (See Proverbs 14:29; Psalm 37:8.) Jesus experienced the full range of human emotions. It is all right for us to feel them, but remember, Jesus resisted Satan's attempts to manipulate Him when He was hungry, lonely, tired, or tempted. Our emotions can be a real part of our perceptions without overriding them.

WHAT ABOUT YOU?

1. List the three things that make you angry.

2. How do you usually react when you are under stress?

3. Now, while you are not angry or stressed, decide how you would like to respond when your emotions are high.

The fourth aspect of what we perceive is interpretation, making sense of what we perceive.

The processes of selection, expectation, and emotional reaction happen so quickly that we are usually unaware of them. We become aware of them at the point that we put it all together into some whole, or gestalt. Interpretation can be challenging. You make selections based on your own interests and background. Your expectations are dictated by your experiences with similar situations. You emotions in different settings play a large role in your perception of people and situations.

No wonder you may understand a situation in a completely different way than someone else! Interpretation is a personal matter but it will help you identify the spots where you may find yourself on the opposite side from someone else. It may help you troubleshoot situations so that you do not end up in misunderstandings that cause problems. It should help you arrive at a fuller, richer understanding by sharing your perceptions with others.

COMMUNICATING AT WORK

You may find yourself in a leadership role where you work. How effective are you? As women have moved into management responsibilities and assumed more visible leadership positions, professional behavior is a must. Regardless of the level of your responsibility, here are three work behaviors that will help you grow as a professional. These behaviors can also help you develop a home-based business, manage your household, or serve as a volunteer in your community or church.

1. **Your expertise matters.** Even your ability to describe your specific job may have an impact on your effectiveness. Describe your job to some friends. They may be able to help you realize what you have omitted. It is important that you are able to verbalize what you do and what you can do.

2. **Your standards and attitudes will be evident.** If you have poor work standards, it will show up in your work product. It isn't enough to know what you do. You need to create a sense of trust with clients and co-workers. If you lead a

community task force, your work ethic will show. Would you have your nails done by a technician who has dirty, broken nails? How about a retail salesperson waiting on you who has missing blouse buttons? Or a coffee barista who berates a co-worker openly behind the counter? You may believe your bad attitude isn't seen by anyone. Think again.

3. **Your communication skills are critical.** Correcting your communication "deficiencies" is an easy fix. Colleges, Christian women's events, conventions, and church training programs offer communication-building seminars. Learning to navigate and manage technological communications is a much-needed, serious component for every leader, for every woman who desires to be successful in her relationships with family, friends, clients, and co-workers. Whether you answer the phones at work, interview prospective employees, lead training workshops, counsel couples, or negotiate contracts, your ability to communicate will determine your success as a twenty-first century leader.

THE ELEPHANT IN THE ROOM: TECHNOLOGY

In an article about women and their cell phones, Time Publishers Inc. said that 60 percent of those surveyed said their smartphones were the most important device in their lives. *Time* called this connection "The Unbreakable Bond." Women were early adaptors to smartphones. Eighty-seven percent of the women said they couldn't imagine life without it, and 88 percent of those surveyed reported they used their phone during their average of 92 minutes of "empty time" per day.

Women readily use their phones for online searches for stores, products, and to post about their purchases. Nearly one half of the women would rather use their smartphone than ask a store clerk questions. Women don't seem to mind getting ads on their phones since they can control the experience. The survey revealed that colorful visuals attract their attention, and it's even better if the offers she receives are based on location.

While these facts illustrate the impact of technology in our personal lives, every other aspect of our lives relies to some extent on expanded technological resources. Our world is more fast-paced than ever before, and we feel pressure to do everything quickly. With Internet online file-sharing services, we can share photos, files, minutes, and proposals, even training manuals! A word of caution, however: as leaders it is very tempting to communicate only by way of technology. When we do that, communication becomes impersonal. If leaders are ineffective in their communication efforts, they may choose to hide behind technology.

Let's face it: with technology it's easier to dispense with worrying about making eye contact! All of us have received emails that are harsh in their wording and cause anxiety and confusion. When communication is limited to the written word, the nuances of nonverbal communication are lost. Those pregnant pauses and silences are missing.

PICTURE THIS

You have written an email to the members of your committee. You wrote it because you were irritated with the way the community project has been going. As you read what you've written, you realize your message can be read in two ways: a terse message telling its readers what to do and how to do it; or, as an expression of disappointment that progress on the project isn't going well and you don't have a solution. Neither is what you really mean to say.

Your intent was to motivate committee members to be more interested in the project's outcome and to work more efficiently. Well, that wouldn't happen if that message were sent! So, with one quick motion you delete the entire email. Because we have the capabilities of sending and receiving communications rapidly, it is tempting to take shortcuts that will "muddy the waters" and create misunderstanding, perhaps even anger, on the part of the receivers.

I once had a boss who would talk about messages he had received that upset him. He'd tell us how he had responded, and then after a brief pause, he'd say, "No, I didn't send it. I hit *delete*!" Peter Bregman in his *18 Minutes: Find Your Focus, Master Distraction, and Get the Right Things Done*, discusses how Gmail is set up to help the communicator control his or her emotions by programming in a five-second delay before a message is sent. This replaces the adage to "take a deep breath and count to 10."

Eric Schmidt, chairman and CEO of Google, told graduates at University of Pennsylvania to, "Turn off your computer. You're actually going to have to turn off your phone and discover all that is human around us."

WHAT ABOUT YOU?

If you have a cell phone device, answer these questions.

1. Do you mind getting advertisements on your phone?

2. How many times a day do you check your messages on your phone? Is the number excessive?

3. Do you use your mobile device to shop? To get directions? To check the weather?

4. Does your device help you at work or only with personal things?

A WORD OF CAUTION

If we agree that technology can both bless and hurt our communication efforts, are there any benefits to embracing all the technology available to us? How did we accomplish anything before the days of smartphones, iPads, emails, Twitter, Facebook, and more? Because of our heavy reliance on it, several things have developed.

Technology is definitely a distraction. As you begin writing the report due tomorrow morning, the fax machine whirrs. You are in the middle of a conversation with a client and your cell vibrates or rings. Contrary to what we would like to think, technology doesn't always improve our productivity. It does, however, raise our expectations. We have come to believe we must be available 24/7. (I can remember when I didn't know what that term meant!) We have the mistaken belief that every text message and email must be answered within 10 minutes.

Last year a situation developed with maintenance of a home we own in another state. I was out of state (a third state!) so had no access to my normal resources. Using my friend's computer, I tried to make arrangements to purchase a new appliance and have it delivered. Being 2,200 miles away is less than the best of scenarios! Finally, after 22 phone calls and numerous emails, a new appliance was delivered. It was then that I decided I had to curb the number of communications I answer daily. My pattern was to answer every message immediately. I can say that now, when my cell pings, I can answer or not and am not terribly bothered by creating a boundary for myself. My 97-year-old mother, however, can't stand for a message to go unread or unanswered for a few minutes as she became used to my scrambling to respond!

Yes, technology can improve our communication, but we must strive to build trust, which technology does not. Building trust is low-tech, high-touch. Think about your use of technology and make adjustments if necessary.

⚞ IMPROVING HOW WE LEAD ⚟

The Old Testament judge Deborah may have wished for an excuse not to lead out at some point, but she was a prophetess and judge in the hill country of Ephraim and the Israelites obviously trusted her, for they came to her to have their disputes settled. For 20 years the Israelites had been oppressed by a cruel military commander, Sisera. Deborah sent Barak specific instructions to lead the way with ten thousand troops to Mount Tabor in order to engage Sisera in battle. Barak agreed to go only if Deborah would go with him. Barak followed Deborah's instructions and defeated Sisera's army. Deborah wrote and sang a song of celebration for the great national victory (see Judges 4–5).

Deborah is a woman who demonstrates the very best principles of an approach to leadership called situational leadership. *Taking into account the needs of the people she was leading, she changed her style in order to help them grow in the tasks she assigned them. Situational leadership, a model developed by Ken Blanchard and Paul Hersey, can give us guidance regarding the communication style to use in a given situation.*

Leaders can be leaders, after all, only if their followers follow them! That means leaders must be carefully tuned in to the needs of their followers (no disconnected numbers!). If a leader meets a person's needs, that person will be extremely loyal. Too often leaders begin to think that followers are supposed to meet the leader's needs.

> *"I must follow the people. Am I not their leader?"*
>
> — BENJAMIN DISRAELI

LOOK OVER YOUR SHOULDER . . . IS ANYONE FOLLOWING?

There is no one perfect leadership or communication approach. What is effective depends on the situation, the needs of the people involved, and the job the leader is asking them to do. The leader must assess the specific task in a given situation and determine the ability and the willingness of the individual or group being asked to accomplish it.

Ability. Is the individual capable of doing the task? Has she ever done it before? Has she been trained? If so, little information or direction is needed from the leader. If not, the worker needs more communication, attention, and assistance from the leader.

Willingness. Is the worker confident of her ability to do the task? Is she comfortable with the assignment? Does she want to do it? If the answers to these questions are yes, the worker needs less encouragement and support from the leader than if any of the answers are no.

~ IMPROVING HOW YOU LEAD ~

Many books discuss the various approaches to leadership, all of which involve specific communication skills. Let's look at four that can be related to the biblical story of the Old Testament judge Deborah.

Telling. *If the individual or group has a low level of ability or willingness, the leader will need to give a lot of emphasis to the task — specific instructions about what needs to be done, when it should be done, how it should be done, and who should do it. This could involve: staying in close touch, setting up frequent reports or meetings, providing manuals with detailed information, pairing a new leader with an experienced one as a model, and setting deadlines.*

Deborah functioned in a telling fashion when she gave Barak specific instructions. Barak evidently was either unwilling or felt unable to accomplish the task alone. In fact, he said he would follow Deborah's instructions only if she went with him. Deborah recognized he would be unable to succeed alone and agreed to go with him (Judges 4:8–10).

Coaching. When an individual or group begins to develop a bit more experience and willingness, the leader can move to a style that is a little less directive and a little more supportive. A coach gives direction but also provides encouragement and support. Encourage those you have asked to take on responsibilities, give them feedback, and use debriefing sessions that include celebration of successes.

Barak became more confident as he and Deborah were followed by ten thousand men. Deborah moved to a coaching style when she urged him, "Go! This is the day the Lord has given Sisera into your hands. Has not the Lord gone ahead of you?" (Judges 4:14).

Encouraging. A group or an individual with a good bit of experience and willingness to do a task is usually eager to have a say in how the task is done. Not needing much instruction or supervision, the leader can facilitate their moving into a leadership role of their own. During the time of Jabin, the evil king of Canaan, Deborah was Israel's leader. My guess is that she used encouragement as a primary style of communication with her people. The people came to her for help in deciding their disputes, and this sounds like she empowered them to be involved in those decisions. After the defeat of Sisera, she joined Barak in a song of great jubilation. She recognized her role in the triumph, but she also paid homage to others who were involved (Judges 5).

Delegating. Truly experienced, capable, and eager individuals or groups are able to take on the responsibility of the task, leaving the leader to spend time on other tasks or with other groups who are at lower levels of ability and willingness. Allow your leaders to *be in charge unless they come to you with requests for assistance.*

Deborah knew from the first that Sisera would be defeated by a woman (Judges 4:9) and was obviously willing to leave that entirely up to Jael. Jael was the wife of Heber the Kenite, from a clan that had peaceful relations with Jabin the king. Sisera clearly went to her because he thought she would provide a safe hiding spot. She didn't hesitate in carrying out her plan to destroy Sisera. Capable of the task, she carried it out without direction or encouragement!

STOP TO EVALUATE

These questions might help you evaluate a project you are working on right now. Evaluation is a critical part of the process because it can clarify unaddressed issues, unspoken needs, or inadequate communication. Think about your answers. Don't simply fill in the blanks!

1. Were the specific goals of this task clear?   Yes ☐   No ☐
2. What specifically made the goal so clear or unclear?
3. Did you have an understanding of what you were supposed to do on this task?
4. What did the leader (or you) do that helped?
5. Did you receive encouragement and support in accomplishing the task?   Yes ☐   No ☐
6. In what specific ways were you encouraged and supported?
7. Next time, what would you suggest to help the leader improve? (Answer this even if you were the leader!)

REMEMBER . . .

☒ *No leader is perfect*, but the most effective leaders remember that people perform best when their needs are met.

☒ *A good leader asks questions and listens* carefully to insure that she can offer the direction and support most needed by her team.

☒ *An effective leader helps* her followers do their very best by choosing the appropriate approach in any given situation.

CAN YOU HEAR ME NOW? LISTENING

The mother went to the back door one more time and called her daughter. No response. She knew she'd been heard. The daughter knew she'd been called. No response. With other more pressing things to do, the mother went about her work and finally, in her own time, the little girl came inside. "Mama, I'd have come if I'd heard you calling!" Hmm. Sounds as if "someone" wasn't listening. She'd heard her mother's voice but didn't really listen.

Listening may be the most important part of communication. It may not have occurred to you that more time is spent in listening than in talking, reading, or writing. Most of us spent a great deal of time learning to read and write. Some of us took speech classes or received some oral assignments. Very few of us have had any formal training in listening. It is through listening that we validate each other. It is through listening that we create the opportunity to truly know each other.

⚜ MARY ⚜

An excellent example of listening is Mary, the sister of Martha and Lazarus of Bethany. It was to their house that Jesus went for fellowship and rest. Martha, the elder of the sisters, took her responsibilities as hostess very seriously. Jesus brought His disciples with Him, so there were a number of people to feed and prepare for. She worked hard getting ready for them, and serving them after they arrived.

Mary was also excited about Jesus' visit. Her focus, however, was on the opportunity to be with Jesus Himself. She was so eager to be with Him that, even though women usually did not sit with men, she joined the group with Him in order to simply listen to what He had to say. After a time, Martha became frustrated with the responsibilities she had assumed and was shouldering alone. She went to Jesus, asking Him to tell Mary to help her. Jesus responded that Mary had chosen the better thing to do, to listen and learn of Him (see Luke 10:38–42).

LISTENER PROFILES

We all know people who are good listeners, and we certainly won't forget the poor listeners we've come across. Here are the profiles of both types:

Good listeners: friendly, open, warm, empathetic, patient, honest, sincere

Bad listeners: closed, impatient, nervous, angry, unwilling to change

Good listening is critical to becoming a good leader. A leader must be aware of the skill level and willingness of people to do various tasks. Through good listening, a leader can have the information necessary to make wise decisions about how best to lead in a given situation.

The following exercises are opportunities to assess your own listening skills, identify some typical listening problems, and work toward increasing listening effectiveness.

HOW WELL DO YOU LISTEN?

Take a few minutes to think about your listening skills. Think about a conversation you've had recently. Then answer these questions as honestly as you can.

1. What were you thinking about as the other person was speaking?
2. Were you really hearing what the person was saying, or were you adding your own interpretation?
3. How do your attitudes about the speaker or the topic of conversation affect your listening skills?
4. How do hidden messages or unspoken communication affect the way you respond in a conversation?

WHAT HINDERS EFFECTIVE LISTENING?

When my oldest son, Wayne, was in elementary school he had an aversion to vegetables, especially green beans. From his point of view, the only good green bean was one on its way to the garbage disposal! When we would try to convince him to eat them at dinnertime, he would hold his fingers in his ears and repeat over and over in a loud voice, "I can't hear you! I can't hear you! I can't hear you!" Certainly an obstacle to listening!

Let's look at several specific areas that may become obstacles to effective listening. We as leaders are well aware that not everything we say is "heard." Why do we know this? Because when we are the listeners, we aren't always receiving the messages either! Selection (what we choose to hear); perception (influenced by our language, backgrounds, experiences, and so on); filtering systems (eliminating what doesn't interest us or what bothers us); emotions, silence, apprehension, and generation issues may severely minimize the messages we receive.

The barriers, or obstacles, come in multiple forms:

Physical conditions may limit listening. Poor lighting, outdated equipment, background noises, external distractions, or visibility issues can create problems for listeners. Your message may be important, and you may be prepared, but results can be limited if the physical environment is unconducive to listening.

Attitudes are critical in how your communication is received. Remember that your attitude is not the only one that needs to be positive! Communication can fail if your staff or organization's attitude is negative. If there is a lack of consultation or if there are personality conflicts, communication will be unsuccessful. When members of a group, task force, or volunteer organization are dissatisfied, communication can fail. One of the greatest causes of miscommunication is insufficient training. As a leader, these attitude issues are ones you should address.

Linguistics may not even be on your radar, but they can be the reason hearing doesn't lead to listening. How clear are your explanations? Are you saying what you mean to say? Do you intentionally plan what you are going to say? This is another area where technology can interfere with effective communication. Reread everything you write in emails or put into reports or proposals, making certain what you are asking or proposing is very clear! Another linguistic issue is our tendency to use jargon that is familiar to us but may be like another language to the listeners.

Physiological conditions may create barriers to effective listening. How well do you listen at the first seminar at a conference after getting off a four-hour plane ride? I attended a large conference several years ago where one of the keynote speakers was obviously "off her game." Her attempts to communicate her ideas failed miserably. Commenting to someone about how disappointed I was in her presentation, I was told she was running a temperature and should have been in bed. Illness will undermine both the communicator and the listener! Obviously hearing or eyesight problems will affect listening also.

TIPS FOR EFFECTIVE LISTENING

1. **Stop talking!** You can't listen if your mouth is open.
2. **Attend as a listener.** In other words, behave as if you are there to hear and learn. Establish eye contact with the speaker. Put a pleasant, interested look on your face. Use nonverbal gestures to indicate you are listening. Give the speaker the time she is allotted. Keep your emotions under control.
3. **Listen for the main points.** Take notes if you have to, to maintain your attention level.
4. **Concentrate.** The speaker deserves your attention.
5. **Be open-minded.** Don't make up your mind ahead of time what the speaker will say and how you will respond. Consider the options and then when you've heard everything, make the decision about what your viewpoint will be.
6. **Watch out for words** that will cause an emotional reaction. All of us have certain words that trigger our emotions. Identify those words, and learn to slow down your response to them. Force yourself to get past the words in order to understand the speaker.

7. **Defer judgment.** Wait until you have heard and are sure you understand the meaning of the whole message before you make any decisions.

8. **Listen empathetically.** In other words, listen from the speaker's point of view, rather than from your own perspective.

9. **Ask questions.** Questions show your interest and encourage the speaker as well as clarify the message for you.

10. **Stop talking!**

❧ COMMUNICATING WITHOUT WORDS ❧

Mary was a listener who instinctively knew the techniques of good listening. She was quiet, responsive, and supportive of Jesus as He spoke and taught. We know that her entire focus was on Jesus, even to the point of forgetting the norms of the times and her responsibilities as a hostess. We know that she listened well and absorbed His meaning, because Jesus commended her.

Dorcas was part of an active Christian community in Joppa, and evidently provided a great deal of leadership in reaching out to minister to the poor. She was known as someone who was always doing good. Dorcas became ill and died. Those who loved her prepared her body for burial and placed her in an upstairs room. Hearing that the Apostle Peter was in Lydda, not too far away, they sent for him, asking him to come at once. Whether they wanted him there because they thought he could perform a miracle, or because he should be there for the burial, we don't know. We do know that Peter went right away.

When Peter arrived at the upstairs room, it was filled with widows, who showed him the robes and other clothing Dorcas had made. After sending everyone out of the room, Peter knelt and prayed. Then he turned to Dorcas and asked her to rise. She opened her eyes and sat up. Peter called everyone back in and presented Dorcas to them. This event became known all over Joppa, and many people believed in the Lord (based on Acts 9:36–42).

Dorcas sent significant messages through her behavior to people who knew her. She gave to others, she did for others, and she cared about people in need. Her life served as a witness to her faith and spoke more loudly to those around her than anything she might have said. Dorcas witnessed nonverbally as she gave of herself to others. Without words, she preached the message of Jesus.

WHAT YOU'RE DOING SPEAKS SO LOUDLY THAT I CAN'T HEAR WHAT YOU ARE SAYING

Researchers in the field of communication claim that nonverbal communication, such as facial expressions and the ways words are said, relay more information than do spoken words. Joyce Mitchell shared these statistics in her book, *Teams Work*, which remain current from selectassesstrain.com: only 7 percent of meaning in a conversation is verbal. That means that 93 percent is nonverbal! Of that 93 percent, tone and inflection (the way words are said) account for 38 percent, with 55 percent being facial expression.

Nonverbal communication covers a host of forms of communication. In fact, it involves so many things that it has been said that we cannot *not* communicate. Think about that for a minute. Even a refusal to communicate communicates something!

Our nonverbal communication often is unintentional. Have you ever had someone come up to you and ask, "What's wrong?" You weren't intending to convey distress, but something about your expression sent that signal. Our clothes, the condition of our desk and office, our housekeeping style, the appearance of our yard, the time we spend in certain activities — these are all ways we communicate whether we intend to or not. Our Christian witness is often the product of unintentional messages. These can be the strongest messages we send!

In this section, we will be looking at the functions of nonverbal communication and at a variety of forms of body language.

TRY THIS

Watch a conversation from a distance. Based on facial expression, body language, and tone of voice (if you can hear the voices), make up what you think the content of the conversation is. What are the attitudes of the persons involved?

HOW DOES NONVERBAL COMMUNICATION WORK?

He looked right at me as I spoke. I made eye contact with the group during my presentation. I shifted my vision back to X, and his eyebrows were raised to new heights. His arms were folded, and he wasn't moving at all. I continued to speak and finally made it through my prepared explanation of a project I was proposing.

There was no verbal response from X. The meeting ended, and I was no closer to understanding if he understood my words, had an opinion, or anything about what he thought of my idea. Communication is full of innuendoes, landmines, and subterfuge. It's a wonder we understand others! Remember the illustration of two persons with a tangled string in-between them?

As we listen to our bosses, members of our groups, committees, or task forces, we rely almost exclusively on what we hear (and hope we comprehend). However, we need to realize that the spoken word is only one part of communication. Perhaps weighing more than words is body language. When we are uncertain what the speaker means, we look at him or her for more information. It is the emotional information that fills in the communication gaps for us.

Carol Fleming, a speech pathologist, discusses that while listeners are fairly good at interpreting the verbal words, voice tonalities and expressions "leak information" of which we may be unaware. We often respond to emotional displays more than the informational content of what someone says. As leaders we must pay attention to the nonverbal messages we send. As listeners, we need to be aware of the same type of messages that impact what we are hearing.

WHAT ARE SOME SPECIFIC WAYS WE SEND NONVERBAL MESSAGES?

1. **The way you carry yourself when you communicate sends a nonverbal message.** Your posture and even the way you dress say something about the value you place on what you are saying. Fiddling with buttons or jewelry sends the

"I'm very nervous" message. Standing tall gives you dignity and conveys "I am confident in what I'm saying." I have a severe curvature of the spine, so I must consciously stand straight, not list to one side, and make an intentional effort not to slump. How you dress for the communication situation is also telling. If your appearance is neat, it shows that you think the occasion is important. A number of years ago I attended a city's historical dinner. The keynote speaker wore baggy pants and no socks. I must admit that his appearance distracted me, almost keeping me from hearing what he said verbally.

2. **How you look when you speak affects your ability to communicate effectively.** All of us are skilled in interpreting the expressive movements of the face. Why do you think large conference halls and auditoriums use overhead screens? We want to see the speakers' faces! Scowling as you speak is distracting; people think something is wrong. Schooling yourself to look pleasant as you talk communicates that you are interested in the subject, in your listeners, and are enthusiastic about being present. Remember: what *you* see in the mirror is not necessarily what *others* see.

3. **Making eye contact is another nonverbal communication.** Even if everyone in your group is intent on looking at their computer screens, tablets, or smartphones, try to make eye contact at some point. Eye contact can be eloquent in several communication situations: when you are striving for interaction with others; if you were to intimidate with a look; or when an intimate occasion is the goal. Eye contact is an emotional communication skill that every leader needs to develop.

Note: In our smaller-than-before world of today, it is important that leaders are aware of cultural differences in personal space. The Additional Reading section at the end of this book gives the titles of several good books on crossing cultures that will be helpful when you find yourself trying to communicate with a person or persons from other cultures.

4. **Showing your interest is critical in communicating effectively as a leader.** From a listening standpoint, stop what you are doing (filing, typing, writing) when someone speaks to you. My father was a pastor, and one thing irritated him more than anything as he visited people in their homes. After being welcomed inside, he spent the entire visit trying to talk over the television they didn't turn off!

5. **Be approachable when you are communicating with others.** Look friendly and nonthreatening. Whether you are communicating through technology, speaking in front of small groups, making presentations for work, or trying to establish a community network, it is critical that you are the type of person people are drawn to.

THINK ABOUT YOUR NONVERBAL COMMUNICATION

Ask a friend to evaluate your nonverbal communication the next time you lead a small group at church, make a project presentation for work, or report on activities of the high school's booster club.

1. What did my voice convey about the message and my feelings about it?
2. How should I try to improve my voice?
3. What did my body language say about me or the message?
4. How could I improve my body language?

5. What did my clothing, accessories, and so on convey about my message or about me?
6. How can I improve my dress, accessories, and so on to send a more positive message?

❦ DID BIBLE WOMEN SPEAK IN PUBLIC? ❧

Consider Dorcas and the nonverbal messages she sent as she sewed for those in need. Did her messages augment her verbal witness? Did they substitute for spoken messages? Or did they contradict her other messages? We don't know a lot about Dorcas's verbal interactions with others. We do know that her behavior spoke for itself. Her behavior complemented her Christian commitment, and it may well have stood on its own as a substitute for more assertive forms of witness. In no way did Dorcas's behavior contradict the Christian principles by which she lived.

ONLY PUT ME OUT OF MY MISERY: NO PUBLIC SPEAKING FOR ME!

The ability to speak articulately and persuasively before a group is one of the more important skills a leader needs. For many people, however, the fear of public speaking is greater than their fears of deep water, financial difficulties, illness, or heights. Before addressing how you can increase and strengthen public speaking skills, let's look at a biblical example of a woman who was articulate and effective in speaking in front of others.

Priscilla and her husband Aquila were Christian tentmakers with a burning missional drive. They welcomed Paul to stay in their home when he left Athens and went to Corinth. Paul, also a tentmaker, felt comfortable with them. He stayed in Corinth for a year and a half, preaching and working with his friends. When he left to go to Ephesus, Priscilla and Aquila sailed with him.

After a time, Paul left them in charge of the church in Ephesus. Their home became the meeting place for the group of Christians. Priscilla and Aquila took a young scholar, Apollos, under their wings, teaching him more fully the truths of Christianity.

Paul's letters to the churches at Rome and Corinth, as well as his letter to Timothy, mention Priscilla and Aquila with great fondness, and he credits them with saving his life (see Acts 18; Romans 16:3; 1 Corinthians 16:19; 2 Timothy 4:19).

These brief pieces of information about Priscilla imply a great deal. In a society in which women were second-class citizens, she is consistently mentioned before her husband. Her name is found on monuments in Rome. Tertullian, an early church father, mentioned her as "the holy Prisca, who preached the gospel." Tradition credits her with a book, the Acts of St. Prisca, and some even credit her with the authorship of the Epistle to the Hebrews. She was, without doubt, a woman able to effectively and persuasively develop a message.

ARE YOUR KNEES KNOCKING YET?

What abilities did Priscilla possess that we as female leaders might develop to become more effective in our public speaking? Before any of us can become a persuasive speaker, we must look at the apprehension we feel when called to make a presentation, lead a workshop, or speak before a group of people.

Many times our fear of speaking comes from experiences in which we have not been effective, clear, or successful in presenting our messages. We have speech habits that are not good ones and speech patterns that contribute to poor communication. This next section may cause you to think about whether you have any of these poor voice or speech behaviors. Mark the ones where you need to improve and follow the suggestions to correct what you may be doing wrong.

1. **You have been told you talk too fast.** If this is something you do, you may be taking shortcuts in articulation that impede understanding on your listeners' part. What can you do about your speaking speed? Try these things: First, take into account the acoustics of the room where you will be speaking. If the sound system is poor (or nonexistent), you will need to adapt your speech speed to facilitate understanding. Second, know the age of your audience. If you are speaking to predominantly senior citizens, take into consideration their needing longer to process what they hear. Third, if there are distractions in addition to your fast speaking rate, the audience may have trouble hearing you. Last, practice slowing down! This will be especially important if you are speaking with a translator.

2. **Think about your voice's volume.** You may discover that you speak too loudly or too softly. If people can't hear you, they can't understand you. Don't rely alone on volume; use energy and motivational statements to work to your advantage.

3. **Be sure the end of your sentences don't fade out.** Pay attention to whether your sentence endings are as strong as their beginnings. No one likes to listen to mumbling speakers!

4. **How dynamic is your speaking voice?** Effective leaders need a voice that shows their confidence and ability. You can practice speaking more dynamically by participating in drama or music presentations. Reading children's books aloud is another good way of speaking dramatically as you assume the role of characters speaking. Use a different voice for each character, vary your reading speed, volume, and use dramatic pauses for emphasis.

I was a member of a church where the minister of education made the announcements in the worship services. He was often told that he'd forgotten to make such and such an announcement. He actually rarely forgot to make them, but his voice was so monotone no one listened to what he was saying! A perfect example of what we must guard against as we speak in front of others.

TRY THIS

Intonation patterns can trip us up as we speak because of the emphasis on syllables. An effective speaker is prepared ahead of time to pronounce the words correctly. Practice using the following words in these sentences or in sentences of your own.

☐ He used his farm to produce vegetable produce.

☐ Did he refuse to dispose of the refuse?

☐ It was time to present the present.

☐ My boss will not object to the object I am proposing we manufacture.

☐ While all the medical records were filed, the nurse hadn't found time to record the final data.

☐ I can't recall which of the cars the automobile maker will recall.

Ask Yourself Some Questions

If you answer yes to any of these questions, you have some work to do to build your public speaking skills.

☐ Are you frequently asked to repeat what you've said?

☐ Do you drop the endings of words? (the "t," "d," or "g")

☐ Do you often have difficulty being heard in noisy situations?

☐ Do you speak with a staccato style?

☐ Does your voice sound breathy?

☐ Is your delivery all in one tone, speed, or volume?

BECOMING A WELL-SPOKEN LEADER

Fair or not, people are judged by the way they speak. As leaders we want to make a good impression on others. You may be retired, a young mother, a church volunteer, a human resource manager, or the coordinator of a major community event. Any of these roles could involve speaking in public. Rather than running from this least-favorite element of leadership, embrace it. Remember these three things:

1. **Work to be articulate.** Words count! *How* we say them counts even more. Choose words carefully, and voice them with conviction and intention

2. **Strive to be fluent.** Avoid overusing flowery speech, such as "really," "just," or "terrific." Empty phrases undermine the impact of your words, and leave the audience feeling you are "fluff." Use real words and develop your vocabulary. Sign up for a daily new word at Merriam-Webster.com, or visit an online vocabulary-building site such as FreeRice.com

3. **Be courteous as you speak.** This means you will be sensitive to your audience and show them respect. Condescending

speech has no place in your life as a leader. When you show courtesy, you will seem more polished and gracious.

ARE YOUR KNEES STILL KNOCKING?

Consider these nervous symptoms. Think about your own nervous symptoms and which ones are present when you are in a public speaking situation.

- Voice (quivering, too fast, too slow, monotone)
- Verbal fluency (stammering, halting, vocalized pauses, speech blocks)
- Mouth and throat (swallowing, clearing throat, heavy breathing, dryness)
- Facial expression (lack of eye contact, eyes everywhere, tense face muscles, twitches, blushing)
- Arms and hands (rigid, tense, fidgeting, shaking hands, hands in pockets or hair, sweaty palms)
- Legs and feet (swaying, shuffling feet, pacing, knocking knees)

If you look back at your various symptoms, you can see that almost all of them are examples of your body trying to work off the excess energy it has generated. Your muscles have tensed in preparation for action. If you have a sinking feeling in your stomach, it is because your body is generating adrenalin and other glandular secretions. When that happens, the process of digestion stops and your stomach contracts, causing the sinking sensation.

It is impractical to talk of eliminating the symptoms of speech apprehension! Your goal should be to control those symptoms.

OTHER SUGGESTIONS TO CONTROL THE SHAKING

Know your own reactions. Look back at the list of nervous symptoms.

- *Develop a plan to deal with each symptom.* If your hands sweat, keep a tissue in your pocket. If your mouth gets dry, have water handy. I attended a large conference to hear an internationally known speaker. He evidently had a dry mouth because he had a breath mint in his mouth during his entire presentation. The trouble was that he continually shifted its position. I felt as if 911 should be on speed dial in case he choked on it! I didn't enjoy the session because I was waiting to call the paramedics!

- *If your legs or hands shake* before a presentation, work off the excess energy. Swing your arms, jog in place, rotate your neck and head. These mini exercises will help you release the nerves.

- *Think about your audience.* What is it you want to tell your audience? What do you want them to learn? It really isn't about you, is it? Capture their attention and work to keep them interested in what you are saying.

- *Use memory aids.* This is my opinion, but I believe the worst thing you can do is to read your presentation word for word. If you have a lot of statistics and numbers, of course it's critical you state them correctly. Make notes (easy to read; in large print) and use them as a guideline for important points.

- *Work to reduce any worries you may have.* Choose your clothing the day before your presentation. (What if the blouse you want is dirty? Or you forgot you tore the hem last time you wore those slacks?) Wear comfortable shoes. Arrive early and check out any equipment you will be using.

Greet people as they arrive so you will see friendly faces in the audience.

- *Practice, practice, practice.* There simply is no substitute for solid preparation — ahead of time. I once sat next to a luncheon keynote speaker who spent the entire mealtime writing notes on sticky notes and putting them on her Bible. Any surprise her presentation was disjointed and ineffective?
- *Look for opportunities to speak.* Yes, you read that right! Experience will help you grow in confidence and skills.
- *Remember God is beside you to support you.*

We've talked about a lot of issues relating to public speaking. You may not be any more inclined to do it than when you first started reading! Hopefully, however, you will remember some of the skills you need because I'm almost certain that at some point you will make a report, answer questions about a project, or volunteer to help with a church or community event. Maybe as a retired person you can give others the benefit of experiences you've had. What a great legacy to teach others!

ONE MORE TRY

The following activities can help develop good voice skills that will make you more at ease in front of groups.

Building Voice Confidence
1. Count to five in your normal speaking voice.
2. Begin again at the same pitch, but lower your voice a tone on each number as you count to five.
3. Count to five again, beginning at your normal tone, and raise your voice a pitch with each number.

4. Read the following passage from the song sung by Miriam, Moses, and Aaron. Follow the changes in pitch as indicated:
   (Normal) I will sing to the Lord, for he is highly exalted.
   (Lower) The horse and its rider he has hurled into the sea.
   (Normal) The Lord is my strength and my song; he has become my salvation.
   (Higher) He is my God and I will praise him,
   (Normal) My father's God, and I will exalt him. (Exodus 15:1–2)

THE AUDIENCE OR THE MESSAGE?

As a speaker, you can concentrate on your message, on yourself, or on your audience. If you choose the message, the content of what you say will take priority over the other two options. You will prepare an interesting, solid presentation that will focus on content and purpose. It's possible that the focus will be on you, the speaker. Knowing your content and delivering it well are important, but the most important element is the audience and how it receives the message. If you really care about your audience, it will show in your presentation and the preparation you do ahead of time.

ANALYZE YOUR AUDIENCE

Ask these questions as you prepare:
✓ What does the audience know about your topic? (Don't talk about what they already know. Challenge them to learn something new.)
✓ What's the audience's attitude about your topic?

✓ Are they present because of the topic?

✓ What is the prevailing attitude of the audience?

Don't be blindsided by these things. Here's an example of something that happened to my daughter-in-law not long ago. The coordinator for an Irish dance chapter, she arranged for a group to perform on the Oregon coast for a group of senior citizens. They were to follow a band who, they were assured, was the "attraction." The dance troupe was secondary in the mind of the event director. When the dancers were given only a small space in which to dance, the senior citizen attendees protested, "We came to see the dancers! Put them on the stage!"

KNOW SOMETHING ABOUT YOUR AUDIENCE'S ATTITUDE

What does the audience know about you?

Provide information about yourself to the person introducing you. Emphasize things you have in common with them.

What do you know about the audience?

Ahead of time find out about age span, gender, cultural identity, family status, economic status, religious affiliation, or political status. This information will help you prepare the content of your message.

THINK ABOUT A SPECIFIC SITUATION

Think about an upcoming presentation you are making or a seminar you are leading. Do you know the answers to these questions?

1. Is there anything special about the day or event? Will the time of day have any impact (will the audience have eaten right beforehand?!)?

2. How many people will be there? Are they present voluntarily?
3. Will you be inside or outside? How will the room be arranged? Will there be a stage, lectern, sound system?
4. Why are they meeting? What is likely to be the general mood or atmosphere?
5. What is the agenda? Where do you fall on the program? Will there be other speakers? What is happening before and after your speech?

Note: If you don't have this information, your knees had better be knocking!

ANALYZE YOUR PRESENTATION

✒ PRISCILLA'S PRESENTATION ✒

There is no question that Priscilla had a clear purpose in mind when she taught, wrote, or preached the gospel. Her purpose was to inform all who would listen about Jesus Christ and to persuade them to take Him into their own hearts and lives. Her work with Apollos is an example of her ability to craft a message to meet the needs of her audience.

Priscilla opened her home to provide a place for people to worship. When necessary, she traveled to spread the gospel. Her message was all-important, and she worked carefully to be sure it reached an audience. Priscilla is an example to us of a communicator who was committed to helping her audience understand the message of God.

TWO WORDS ABOUT YOUR MESSAGE

There are two critical elements of your message. It doesn't matter whether you are presiding at a meeting, presenting at a seminar, bringing a report at work, or speaking at a women's retreat. These elements—*purpose and organization*—will "make or break" your effectiveness as a communicator. Let's concentrate now on developing the message. The process is the same whether the message is spoken or written.

Purpose.

A clear purpose for any effort you make at communication is critical. If you don't know what you want to accomplish, how can your listener have any hope of getting there with you? The more specifically you state your goal to yourself, the better you are able to plan and develop your communication.

There are five major purposes for a written or spoken piece of communication:

☒ *To inform*—Informing is the cornerstone upon which the other purposes build. You must make the message easy to understand, easy to remember, and easy to use. The goal: a meeting of the minds, a sharing of understanding on the topic at hand

☒ *To persuade*—In general, persuasion is designed to convince someone to do or to believe a specific thing. The goal? To move an audience from where they are to a new spot, literally or figuratively.

☒ *To entertain*—Entertainment helps an audience relax and enjoy the experience. The goal: to help the audience escape from reality.

☒ *To inspire*—Inspiring asks for a higher degree of devotion or involvement. The goal: to call the audience to greater enthusiasm and to fulfill the commitments they have made.

☒ *To call to action*—After establishing a need, the solution is presented in the form of action. The goal: to move the audience to immediate, specific action.

Organization is the second element.

A carefully organized presentation is always easier to remember than one that isn't organized. The side benefit is that it is easier for you, the speaker, to remember as well. You will feel much more comfortable delivering a well-crafted message than a loose, rambling one.

As you put a presentation together, you might want to consider some of the suggestions that author and speaker Carol Kent makes.

Discover an idea. Ideas are all around you! You may choose an idea based on your knowledge of the audience or to match a theme or even a season. (If your topic has been decided for you, the steps that follow are the same as if you had control over the subject matter.)

Determine your aim or purpose. What matters the most is, did the audience get the speaker's point? If not, their time—and yours as speaker—has been wasted.

Gather information. You cannot shortcut this step! Use libraries, newspapers, reports, and so on as you begin formulating the body of your presentation or speech.

Develop an outline. This step is critical because it will determine your effectiveness as a presenter. Kent says to start with a bang!

Your first twenty-five words should be so well planned that you seize the attention of your audience. Within the first thirty seconds of your talk, the people in the audience have already decided if it's worth their time to listen to you.

Use good transitional statements. Use questions, and statements to move the audience to the next point of your outline.

Establish rapport with the audience. This can be done through humor.

Use appropriate illustrations. These can come from personal experience, reading, or research.

Application is important. Look for spiritual applications as you speak or write.

Develop a strong conclusion. Answer the question, Where do I want to leave the audience?

Pray for God's guidance. Do this before doing any of the above!

As a Woman Speaker, What Should I Know?

Kent believes there are specific guidelines for platform appearance. While she doesn't dwell on attire, she points out that a speaker should find out what the audience will be wearing. It is always fitting to be dressed a bit more formally than your listeners. She gives the following tips especially for women:

⊠ Avoid the "sleeveless" look. No floral, striped, or "cute" dresses.

⊠ Stay away from tight-fitting clothing, see-through materials, skirt slits, and so on.

☒ Be conservative with jewelry. Avoid bangle bracelets or dangle earrings.

☒ Makeup should bring life to your face but not be heavy.

☒ Pay attention to your hair. Does it need a trim?

☒ Wear stylish but comfortable shoes.

☒ Carry an attaché case or purse, but never both.

WOMEN OF GOD: LEADERS WHO COMMUNICATE EFFECTIVELY

Abigail, Deborah, Mary of Bethany, Dorcas, and Priscilla were all women who used their talents in the service of God. All were leaders who used their talents. Central to the leadership each demonstrated was her communication skills. From quiet Dorcas to insightful Abigail to impulsive Mary, these women communicated their commitment in their own unique ways.

You also have talents to be used by God. You are a leader in a variety of ways: at home, at work, with friends, in your community, in your church, in your small group, and so on. You are always communicating. Everything you do says something about who you are and your relationship to God.

Effective leadership and communication involve skills that must be learned and practiced. They do not happen automatically. Involve others and work together to improve the ways you interact with each other.

My prayer is that this chapter has helped you become more effective in how you communicate and lead. You are a woman of God, gifted to serve. May you use your skills and talents in His will!

"Surely whoever speaks to me in the right voice,
  him or she I shall follow,
As the water follows the moon, silently with fluid
  steps, anywhere around the globe."

— WALT WHITMAN

2 RELATIONSHIP ESSENTIALS

By Roberta McBride Damon

THE TAPESTRY OF RELATIONSHIPS

I recently met a woman who is a weaver. She owns seven looms, spins her own thread, and has a wealth of experience in this time-honored textile art. I asked her to give me some basic information about the weaving process, thinking that I might see a connection between the homespun art, me the writer, you the reader, and God in the way He weaves our relationship experiences into rich, meaningful, and beautiful life tapestries.

The longer Adorie talked the more I understood that weaving is not only a process but also one that demands knowledge, skill, and patience. She said several things that I believe we can apply to our relationships, and I hope you'll see them, too, as this chapter unfolds.

Attention to details is critical. The thread chosen for the warp, or the worker threads, must be strong or the final product will not last. The weaving will only be as strong as its weakest thread. The bottom side of the weaving doesn't show;

all the color and special threads are on top. I think this, too, relates to the relationships you and I form. I asked Adorie if you can correct or mend a hole that occurs if the pattern's specific sequence is not followed. She replied, "Once you see the hole, you have to decide whether to unweave the piece or if you can let it go." I have to say that my immediate thought was, *Do I need to let some relationships go?* I asked Adorie about what type of yarn she can use in her weaving. The term *fleece* applies to anything from an animal: sheep, goat, alpaca. And you can even spin gold! Spinning can form "lumps," which will add texture to the woven piece.

As we ended our conversation, my friend made a great statement: "When thinking about texture and pattern, if a weaver veers from the pattern, nothing is ever as good as the original plan or pattern." Does that remind you of a Bible verse? What about Jeremiah 29:11?

Relationship is an elemental thread. We live out our lives within the context of relationships. Beginning with conception in our mother's womb, our very existence extends from the joining of two people in relationship. Our lives as infants and small children depended on the relationships we had with our primary caregivers. As we grew into children, the socialization process continued with playmates and schoolmates. We learned to tolerate. We learned to share. We learned that other people's needs are at least as important as our own. We might not like it, but we find it necessary to give up the infantile idea that the world revolves around us. We discover that we are not the center of the universe after all. What a shock to learn that there are other people to consider.

Over a life span, relationships come to us in multiple sizes and shapes. Each one is like a swatch of fabric that makes up a crazy quilt—triangles, squares, and rectangles. The colors are vivid or muted. The patterns and textures represent an almost infinite variety—stripes, tweeds, plaids, checks, and solids. No two are alike. The threads that stitch them together are the events, experiences, attitudes, and memories that comprise our lives.

Some of our relationships will last forever while others are of short duration. In some we invest our time and energy and love. In others we maintain emotional distance. An acquaintance is different from a friendship, and a friend can be as close as a sister. The quality of the relationship depends on the depth of our investment.

The best relationships are dynamic. They change over time. Your relationship with your parents changed through your growing-up years. Your parents do not relate to you today in the same way they did when you were a child. Sometime during the young adult years, the contract between parents and their grown children is renegotiated. Marriages also change over the course of many years. The marital relationship changes from the honeymoon phase, through life's crises, and into vintage mellowing. If we are wise, our relationships with our sisters and brothers evolve from childhood rivalry into adult caring and sharing. Likewise, friendships are formed and either grow, endure, or fade away.

The quality of relationships change as our lives change. Relationships change by choice or through neglect. They change because we are not the same people at 50 that we were at 20. Relationships also change as our needs change. Sometimes they end because something as simple as our address changes. Though we may be nostalgic about the good old days, we cannot go home again, and having left, the relationships may endure, but we are different because we are no longer children.

Relationship is the stuff of which life is made. We cannot separate ourselves from it. Our primary relationship is with God in whom we live and move and have our being.

How skilled a pastry maker are you? I watched my mother a thousand times as she mixed pastry dough with her hands. She knew by feel when it was right, and she never missed; her piecrust was perfect every time. We have a piecrust relationship with God. All things hold together within that relationship and God never makes a mistake. With God, we have the only perfect relationship we'll ever experience on this earth—no thanks to us. It is God who is the same yesterday, today, and forever (Hebrews 13:8)—gracious, dependable, loving, and forgiving. We may change but He doesn't!

Relationship is basic to our existence. As children, we learn day by day that we are valuable and that others have worth. We learn to get along with people not like ourselves. Our lives are made up of all those who influence us over the years and bring us memories—loving or painful. Each phase of our lives brings new associations. Some old friends move off center stage as new friends move on. Change is part of life. Sometimes we seek it; sometimes we avoid it. Sometimes it simply goes with the territory as a result of our decisions. Even as we deal with the trauma that change inevitably brings, we find our stability in a relationship with the unchanging God.

This chapter focuses on how we relate to others, why relationships are important to us, and how you can enrich the relationships you have with your family, friends, co-workers, and fellow believers. Technology will appear again, and we'll look at how it is impacting our relationships. Women's lives are ever-changing. Changes come as they move from teenage years to college students. More changes come if they marry and perhaps have children. Other changes such as moving, divorce, death of a spouse, and career choices happen. Soon, there are precious grandchildren and the wonderful (?) retirement years!

HEALTHY RELATIONSHIPS

Let's do some "needlework" on the tapestry of our relationships and see what designs emerge. No leader can afford to ignore the dimension that relationships bring to her own life, nor to the lives of those with whom she lives, loves, and works.

WHAT DOES THE WORD MEAN?

Re-la-tion-ship: the state of being related by kindred, affinity, or another alliance; the mutual exchange between two people or groups who have dealings with one another.

List words that end in the suffix -*ship*.

_____ ship
_____ ship
_____ ship
_____ ship
_____ ship
_____ ship

You may have thought of *fellowship, courtship, friendship, partnership, kinship, guardianship, dictatorship, governorship, authorship, readership,* or others. All have to do with relationship.

The suffix *-ship* means "ability" or "capability," so that friendship means "the ability to be or the capability of being a friend." *Courtship* means "the ability to court." *Worship* literally means "the ability to be of worth."

Re-la-tion-ship means "the ability to relate," or to have mutual exchanges. It implies giving and receiving, initiative and respectful distance, mutuality, and cooperation. Relationship has to do with "one anothering."

One way we describe various relationships is by using the language of physiology. *Face-to-face* indicates interaction between two people. When we see two people face-to-face, we do not immediately know the nature of the interaction. If we say two people see *eye-to-eye*, we mean that there is agreement in certain matters. If, however, we say two people are *eyeball-to-eyeball*, our impression may be that there is confrontation. Other phrases that describe confrontation or combat are *nose-to-nose, toe-to-toe, hand-to-hand,* or *head-to-head.* The French term *tête-à-tête* is more akin to the English *cheek-to-cheek,* or *arm-in-arm,* which denote romance. *Heart-to-heart* and *hand-in-hand* are terms that conjure up notions of love, talk, bonding, and friendship. *Mouth-to-mouth* is associated with life-saving resuscitation. *Neck-and-neck* denotes equality and competition. As you think about relationships, be aware of the nuances both in definitions and in the reality of the relationships themselves.

HOW IMPORTANT ARE RELATIONSHIPS?

A person's early experiences determine the ability to establish relationships with others. I'm sure you've read accounts of a child's problems due to "failure to thrive," which can be caused by lack of attention and love as a baby.

Past relationships provide a person with the confidence to explore the world and help the individual cope with stress and other life demands. How a person deals with disappointment and loss can be determined in part by the relationships she or he has. Making sense of her own world and the outside world are impacted by the type of relationships she has in her life, as well as the ones in her past.

HOW DO RELATIONSHIPS HAPPEN?

Sometimes a relationship simply happens, such as those from *kinship*. However, because you were born of the same parents does not automatically guarantee that you will relate well to each other.

Many relationships are *intentional*, due to a mutual decision, either spoken or by tacit agreement. Two people have to decide to invest themselves to a degree in their dealings with each other.

Relationships may be anything from an acquaintance to a casual friendship to a best friendship. We have acquaintances, friends, and best friends. Romantic relationships fall into another category altogether.

Geography may determine how much contact you have with another person, but deep and meaningful relationships often extend over time and distance. I have a friend who lives in another state, which means that we don't often get to see each other. But, when we do see each other or talk on the phone, it's as if no time has passed, and the 2,200 miles separating us are shoved into the background.

A LOOK AT SPACE ISSUES

In our society there are unspoken but clearly understood distances people maintain in various settings. We begin to relate to another person by the simple act of looking. When the person looks back, eye contact is made and a relationship begins.

Intimate space: Intense activities take place here. Whispers, kisses, hugs, comfort, and so on are given in intimate spaces. People in intimate space are touching or they are relating with very little literal space between them, usually never more than a foot-and-a-half apart.

Interpersonal space: Less intimate conversations occur here between friends. Touch is more limited, and speech takes the form of a normal conversational tone. Distance between people here is between one-and-a-half and four feet.

Social space: More formal interchanges take place in this space. These are typical interactions between business associates, customers with service people, and strangers in conversation. The physical distance here is 4 to 12 feet.

Public space: When your pastor is preaching from the pulpit, his voice is geared to reach a congregation, and while he may have a warm tone, the exchange is not personal. Teachers or politicians who lecture are within the public space. When you call a greeting to a neighbor, you are within the public space. Public space means speaker and listener are more than 12 feet apart.

The setting dictates how we relate to another person. Cultural considerations also come into play. If two North

American women friends are conversing, they will sit or stand at a distance that is understood to be comfortable for both. They will look each other in the eyes, and it is permissible for one or the other of them to touch the arm of the person with whom they are talking. If the nationality is changed from North American to Northern European or British, the distance is automatically widened, and there will be less touching. If the two women conversing are Latin American or Mediterranean, they will likely converse more demonstratively and the distance between them narrows to inches.

If we take away either of the women and add a man, the whole equation changes. In every culture, when women and men are interacting, there are understood taboos concerning touching, distance, eye contact, and body posture. Contrary to popular opinion, in male to female interaction, men talk more than women do. Men are more likely to interrupt women than they are to interrupt men.

In public, if personal space is invaded by a stranger, people employ distancing tactics to indicate an unwillingness to be engaged in conversation: a closed facial expression, feigned sleep, reading, turning the body slightly away from the other person, staring into space, using earphones. These are clear signals that a person is staking out personal space, even in a crowd.

HOW WOMEN RELATE: IS IT DIFFERENT?

Numerous books have been written about women's relationships in an attempt to dissect how they work, what they do for women, and if there are noticeable gender differences. Women are interested in how their relationships work (or don't work), how they can improve them, and if they are meaningful to them. I looked on the Internet using "women and their relationships," and my search revealed that a lot of people are interested in women's relationships!

Here are some other issues I found relating to women. I found books and articles on how depression in women is related to anger in their relationships. Connections are a source of psychological health for women. The effect of social relationships on the well-being of women has been studied. What happens when a woman with no social relationships has breast cancer? What are the benefits of mentoring relationships? What can intercultural relationships mean to a woman? Research has been done on how rape and abuse affect women's relationships. What do relationships between older men and younger women look like? Are there any correlations between a woman's religious beliefs and her psychological well-being?

See what I mean? Women are concerned about all their relationships in all the areas of their lives! Stereotypically, women have been characterized as dependent, overly emotional, weak, flirtatious, talkative, shallow, and jealous while men have been labeled as cold, distant, unemotional, aggressive, controlling, and ruthless. Both women and men can be any or all of these things. Therefore, women can be:

☒ selfless yet assertive
☒ meek yet strong
☒ modest yet confident
☒ calm yet effective
☒ kind yet firm
☒ flexible yet responsible
☒ givers yet receivers

☒ listeners yet talkers
☒ learners yet teachers.

WEAVING A STRONG FOUNDATION

As my weaver friend emphasized the importance of using strong thread for the weaving's base, a woman must establish relationships in her life that are supportive, lasting, and healthy. It is valuable to take a backward glance at our relationships in order to understand why some decisions and choices have been made. Use the following profiling exercise as a way of looking into your past.

Fill in the blanks with the first thought that comes to your mind.

1. When I was a child I always wanted to _____
2. My father and I _____
3. My mother and I _____
4. One thing I remember is _____
5. If I could do anything I wanted I would _____
6. One thing that makes me laugh is _____
7. I get angry when _____
8. I am impatient with _____
9. Religion in my life is _____
10. I love _____
11. The thing I most fear is _____
12. I have fun when _____
13. Intimacy is _____
14. I hate _____
15. Something that is important to me is _____
16. I laugh when _____

17. I have the ability to _____

18. One thing I like about me is _____

19. One thing about me I would like to change is _____

20. God is _____

21. My church is _____

Due to her past experiences and choices, a woman may establish relationships that are unhealthy, and they can become detrimental to her. Like my friend said, "If a weaver uses cheap thread for the foundation, she's asking for trouble!" The old children's song about the wise man and the foolish man is still true. Matthew 6:19 speaks about paying attention to what we treasure and that "thieves will break through and steal."

In order to establish connection with others at work, where we live, or at church, we need to have an understanding of what a healthy relationship looks like. Following is a comparison between healthy and unhealthy relationships that you might find helpful as you analyze your own relationships and lead others to learn about theirs.

> *"Their [women's] reliance on close, personal connections gives them a reliable source of trustworthy advice, a bulwark against depression and an enduring foundation for building a happy and fulfilled life."*
> — GRANT SCHNEIDER, *SHE MEANS BUSINESS*

WHAT MAKES A RELATIONSHIP HEALTHY?

In order for you to be an effective leader, you need to understand the characteristics of a healthy relationship. In your leadership role you will be confronted with personality differences, conflict situations, and women who need to make changes in their relationships. Your success in leadership will depend largely upon on how well you grasp the intricacies of relationship within and outside your place of business, family, community, or church.

On a human level, there is no perfect relationship, but good, solid, healthy relationships *do* exist. Three elements are present in a healthy relationship.

1. **Mutuality**—A relationship cannot exist within one person. Relationship implies interchanges between or among people. Two people or groups of people either desire or are forced to relate one to another. Two women may choose to be in a friendship. Two other women may be co-workers who find that they are in daily contact and must work together. Whether you find yourself in a friendship by choice, or in a working relationship by chance, mutuality and cooperation are necessary.

2. **Initiative**—Someone has to make the first move. If you are gregarious, you may find it easy to initiate conversations, plan activities, and do most of the talking and maintenance work on a relationship. If you are more quiet and retiring, this may be difficult to do, as you prefer to wait for the other person to initiate. Since much of life requires interaction, we must all seek to meet each other halfway.

3. **Respect**—Keeping a respectful distance is a necessary ingredient for any healthy relationship. Being considerate of the other person's personal space is important. There is an invisible line in any relationship that marks the division between what is permissible and what is intolerable. We

need to ask permission, wait to be invited, and otherwise be respectful of the rights of other people.

COMPARING HEALTHY AND UNHEALTHY RELATIONSHIPS

HEALTHY RELATIONSHIPS	UNHEALTHY RELATIONSHIPS
There is personal emotional responsibility.	Your feelings are ignored.
Kindness, acceptance, compassion, and empathy are present.	Other person is unkind, lacks empathy and compassion.
Warmth, affection, laughter, and fun can be seen.	There's no warmth or affection returned.
Enjoying time together and apart are important.	Well-being depends on being together all the time.
You learn through conflict.	Other is always right and doesn't listen.
Trust is present.	Suspicious of other's motives and actions.

HOLES IN OUR TAPESTRIES

It could be that you have relationships in your life that are unhealthy; these are holes in your weaving. Perhaps you need to unweave or let them go! As we mature, change, and develop new interests, not all of our friendship relationships will survive. When we change careers or workplaces, many work relationships will cease. As family members die, those kinship relationships also die.

Your responses to the questions below will provide a fairly accurate picture of who you are and in which directions you need to grow in your relationships.

1. *What do you fear?* People are paralyzed by fears—fear of failure, fear of not being good enough, fear of loss, fear of abandonment, fear of death, fear to the point of phobia. Fear prevents normal, healthy functioning. The message of the gospel is the antithesis of fear. "Do not be afraid," said the angel to the shepherds (Luke 2:10). "Do not be afraid," said Jesus, walking on the water toward His frightened disciples (Mark 6:50). "My peace I give to you" (John 14:27).

2. *What makes you angry?* Do you have a short fuse or a long one? Do you tend to explode or simmer? Do you take your anger out on someone not directly responsible for it? Are you aware of long-term anger you carry? Are you mad at the world? Biologically, anger is nothing more than energy. It is an emotion that people find inconvenient at best and devastating at worst.

   Ask yourself, *Do my emotions control me and dictate my behavior, or do I control my emotions?* We cannot help the way we feel; our feelings are valid. We can begin to control the way we think. We can control our behavior. We do have choices.

3. *How do you express affection?* Some people are comfortable expressing affection by their actions. Doing kind things is a legitimate way of saying, "I care about you." These are often overlooked or misinterpreted expressions of affection. You may be comfortable with physical expressions of affection. You may, however, be uncomfortable with a verbal or physical expression of love. Physical

affection may make you uneasy. Because the expression of affection has become sexualized in our society, people tend to be wary of any expression of affection for fear of being misunderstood or sued.

Gender differences play an important role in our attitudes toward the expression of affection. Within the marriage relationship, men tend not to separate sexual expression from love, while women tend to believe love and sex are quite different. Obviously, expressing affection for a husband, a friend, a child, or a parent will differ. One of the marks of a healthy, functioning family is the ability to distinguish among these differences.

4. *What wounds you?* We are wounded by harsh words, hateful looks, or cold silence, if not by rape, incest, or battering. We are also wounded by caustic humor, sarcasm, or ridicule. Some people are so well defended against pain that they literally cannot feel it. While women have been granted the right to weep, weeping is seen almost universally as a sign of weakness.

5. *What makes you laugh?* The benefit of humor in our lives is well documented. We choose our humor style: slapstick, puns, jokes, quirky twists of phrases, and so on. Laughter has been called "the saving grace," "internal jogging," and "the best medicine." It is true that when we laugh, our bodies release *endorphins* into the bloodstream that have a measurable positive effect on our health. It also serves as the lubricant that enhances our relationships. Laughter helps us endure the pain of life. Healthy humor helps us maintain a positive outlook on life. We miss the point if we miss the laughter.

6. *What is important to you?* What are your priorities? What do you value? The answers to these questions give insight into your personality, as moral, ethical, and religious considerations come into play. On a less basic plane, personal tastes and preferences need to be considered.

Compare your answers to the characteristics of healthy and unhealthy relationships. Do you notice any major discrepancies?

Can you handle one more reflection activity?

Read through the true-or-false statements below to see how assertive you are as a person. If your answers reveal a lack of assertiveness, your relationships at home, in the workplace, in your community, and at church will reflect that.

As a woman develops and deletes relationships from her life, she will find that God has a plan for her life and will direct her movements through what we sometimes feel are landmines ready to hurt us. Part of weaving our relationship tapestry is unweaving or letting go! Take a look at yourself by answering these questions.

☐ T   ☐ F   I hesitate to call a friend for fear she may not want to talk to me.

☐ T   ☐ F   When I have a strong opinion about something, I don't hesitate to express it.

☐ T   ☐ F   I think of myself as lacking in self-confidence.

☐ T   ☐ F   If someone doesn't do a good job, they should be fired and replaced.

☐ T   ☐ F   I sometimes feel I'm not worthy of affirmation from others.

☐ T ☐ F I discipline myself.

☐ T ☐ F I don't like the way I look.

☐ T ☐ F I think everyone should follow the same rules.

☐ T ☐ F I sometimes feel I have nothing to say that is worth hearing.

☐ T ☐ F I see myself as more often right than wrong.

☐ T ☐ F I sometimes think of myself as stupid.

☐ T ☐ F People should either do their work or get out of the way and let someone else do it.

☐ T ☐ F I believe other people have more to contribute than I do.

☐ T ☐ F I get angry when I have to wait in line.

☐ T ☐ F I am often depressed.

☐ T ☐ F I am often irritable.

☐ T ☐ F I don't want to intrude on others.

☐ T ☐ F I consider myself a person of high energy.

☐ T ☐ F I am often tired.

☐ T ☐ F I believe in "telling it like it is."

ADDING TEXTURE AND PATTERN

Life wouldn't be life without relationships, would it? Even though there are days (maybe months or years) when we shake our heads and wonder how we can repair, deal with, or survive some of them, our lives would be desolate without them. The health of our connections will impact our attitudes at work, how we regard those different from us, and our ability to support and contribute to others' lives.

Part of the texture of our tapestries is the variety that each relationship holds. No two of our relationships are the same nor do we behave in the same way in each of them. At work you may be one of many employees; or, you might be the CEO. Your relationships at home may be a tangled mess that threatens your well-being. Relationships with other community volunteers may be unproductive, and yes, even your relationships in the faith community might be strained.

As stressful as some relationships can be, they still can bring variety to our lives and add texture to our woven tapestry. This texture comes in many forms through our families, the workplace, friendships, or association with others in the community or at church. Regardless of how many relationships you have formed, each will have its own boundaries, challenges, and benefits. Let's take a general look at some of the contrasts that can exist and then look specifically at friendships and the workplace. Variety is *the spice of life!*

CONSIDER THESE STATEMENTS:

☒ Some people view life as extreme opposites (good or bad; win or lose).

☒ Some persons need time alone.

☒ Some individuals are precise and methodical.

☒ Some are rule-followers and policy-oriented (do not "play it by ear").

☒ Some people are visionaries (others are dreamers).

☒ Some are sensitive and tender-hearted while others put aside personal feelings.

☒ Some persons want to make close emotional attachments.

We have all been in groups, on committees, and worked with people whose personalities are greatly different from ours. They may be shy, independent, warm, or assertive. Their personal styles will affect how they function within their relationships. It is easy to see how this will impact how you as a leader are able to move your group or task force forward to reach its goals.

THE TEXTURE OF OUR FRIENDSHIPS

For women, friendships are critically important. Friendships are priceless! What are some traits that healthy friendships share? Here are a few.

✓ **Good friends are real and honest.** In a healthy friendship you can be the best version of yourself. A true friend won't lie to you but won't be afraid to share their real opinion.

✓ **Good friends can talk through disagreements.** Honest communication will dispel tension and the friendship can move forward.

✓ **A healthy friendship will encourage other connections.** Time apart is a good thing.

✓ **Trust is critical for a healthy friendship.** Sharing, encouraging, and confidentiality cement the relationship.

✓ **Good friends respect each other's boundaries**, which leads to a balanced friendship.

✓ **A healthy friendship nurtures both** participants in a variety of ways.

MY FRIENDS AND ACQUAINTANCES

Complete the exercise below to help you realize that your friends form a network that supports you.

List five persons you consider close to you. Indicate which two are the closest.

1.

2.

3.

4.

5.

List your social network. This could be as many as 15–30 persons (including aunts, uncles, cousins, co-workers, church friends, and so on).

You can probably name 100 to 1,000 acquaintances. Name 5 here (the mailperson, the person at the supermarket, and so on).

1.

2.

3.

4.

5.

THE TEXTURE OF WORK RELATIONSHIPS

According to Gallup business consulting researcher and best-selling author Tom Rath (*Vital Friends*), one significant outcome from review of eight million surveys on Gallup's worldwide database: people who have a good friend at work are seven times more likely to be engaged and satisfied in their jobs! These people are more likely to be creative and innovative and go along with changes. Because we are social creatures, we want positive interactions with others. If you are, or want to become, a leader in your workplace and to advance in your career, good relationships will be necessary. Building and maintaining good relationships with customers, suppliers, and upper management are essential.

What makes work relationships healthy? Again, trust ranks very high on the list of successful relationships in the workplace. Mutual respect creates an environment that values everyone's input and ideas. Being mindful of words and actions impacts others in a positive way. Welcoming diversity is a step to considering others' perspectives. Open communication that is honest will foster strong relationships at work.

LEADING AT WORK

Simply put, you have to work to establish healthy relationships in the workplace! A formerly popular British television series, *Doc Martin*, was the ongoing story of a taciturn physician forced to leave a surgery practice and move to a small fishing village because of a blood avoidance phobia. The series revolved around his inability to establish any type of healthy relationship. I couldn't help but think of "Poor Doc" when I began to read what others have written about the elements necessary for healthy work relationships. Doc's great deficiency was that he had no healthy relationships, and he did not care!

Developing people skills is critical. It is well worth it to take a brief quiz to assess your skills in dealing with others. You may search online to find a quiz you would like to take.

Take time to build relationships. Even a small block of time can help you make lasting connections with your co-workers. Again, Doc was too busy to learn anything about those who come to him for medical treatment. Going to lunch with co-workers, sitting, and talking will be time well-invested.

Everyone wants to feel they are appreciated and valued. Be genuine and you'll be rewarded with some healthy relationships. Doc's receptionist yearned to move beyond doing the mundane duties of her job, but Doc gave no encouragement, no support, no recognition of her efforts.

Avoid gossip. Enough said.

Be positive about as many issues as you can. No one wants to spend time with a negative and complaining person. Doc's prickly attitude drove even the most determined villager away.

Learn to be an active listener. This means that you make it a habit to listen more than you talk. Hearing what others have to say is critical in dealing with unhappy customers or employees.

SO, ARE YOU ADDING TEXTURE TO YOUR TAPESTRY?

This question requires some serious thought. God intends for our lives to be enriched through relationships. Of course, when we detour from His plan, our relationships can become messy and harmful. That's not to say that all of our relationships are within our control as mentioned before. To the best of our ability, however, we can make our work relationships strong and healthy.

THE DETAILS OF WEAVING OUR TAPESTRIES

We have looked at the foundation, holes, and texture of our weaving. We have all this information, but what do we do with it? When I was talking to my weaver friend, she made another comment that I thought was very interesting. "Weaving isn't for everyone because some people can't handle the precision that is involved. Attention to detail is critical." I immediately related her statement to how we establish and maintain our relationships, no matter what they are. The filters we choose, the decisions we make, and the life paths we take are those all-important details.

Do we have to be like Doc Martin, stumbling through life without any positive, encouraging relationships or are there some things we can learn to relate better? We want friendships; work relationships are important; our family connections are complicated. Work through the following suggestions and develop a plan of action to help you build healthier relationships for a richer, more meaningful life.

1. Recognize your own value. This has to happen first. Read *Found Treasures: Finding Your Worth in Unusual Places.*
2. See the value of relating well to others. (Remember Doc?)
3. Recognize the value and worth of others. Look to Jesus as your role model.
4. Develop social skills. Listening, reading, learning, and communication are involved.
5. Ask for what you need from those who can give it. This isn't selfish! Many women will neglect their own needs and put everyone else's ahead of their own legitimate ones.
6. Be willing to cooperate. Is your attitude a cooperative one?
7. Learn how to affirm others.
8. Lead with your strengths and allow others to lead in theirs.
9. Learn how to set healthy limits in your relationships.

Everything on this list can be learned and applied! You can find good books at your local library. The Internet is a wealth of resources for you. Colleges have courses on some of these topics. Contact churches in your community to see what seminars and conferences they offer for women.

SPINNING FOR WEAVING

One last thing about weaving. Not long ago I attended a textile festival. I don't know what I was expecting, but I immediately realized I was way out of my comfort zone! After I met the alpacas and llamas on the lawn, I ventured inside to visit the booths displaying a wide variety of yarn. At least, I think it was all yarn! There were boxes and baskets overflowing with natural and brightly dyed yarn. Some was smooth and soft; other packages were lumpy and neutral in color. I saw looms and spinning wheels (unfortunately not in use). No one offered to educate me, but then, I didn't even know enough to ask questions. I needed Adorie with me!

Adorie spins a lot of her own weaving material so when I talked with her I was able to ask some of the questions I'd had at the festival. *Fleece* is defined as anything that comes from an animal, so yes to the alpacas and llamas out front. Yes to cashmere from goats and wool from sheep. Do you know that Rumpelstiltskin could have really spun gold! You can spin virtually anything, even gold. Hmm, sounds like another application to our discussions about relationships.

Use the following questions to help you focus on what kind of relationships you are "spinning." Maybe they are lumpy or have no color when they could be bright and cheerful. Maybe one or two of them are rough in texture and hinder the quality of your life or perhaps you have spun gold! Good relationships are pleasing in God's eyes, giving your life tapestry beautiful colors and texture. Only you can answer the questions. Be honest in assessing your spinning. Look especially to relationships you have as a leader.

1. How would you rate your use of nonverbal language?
2. How do you sustain your relationships?
3. When you must work with a difficult person, what is your approach?
4. How well do you use humor in your leading relationships?
5. Do you "deny," "dump," "flee," or "fight" in any of your relationships?
6. How do you handle stress in your relationships? (home, work, church, volunteer)

With weaving terms swirling through my head, I ended my conversation with Adorie. *Warp*, *waft*, *shuttles*, *harnesses*, *overshot*, *patterns*, and *looms*. A complicated process, this tapestry-weaving! Like weaving, the foundations and spinning we do for life's relationships must be of quality and strong. Texture is added by the decisions we make as individual women. Remember Adorie's warning about following the pattern? When we deviate from God's pattern, holes appear in our tapestries. We have to learn to let go or unweave (not an easy thing to do). Above all, attention to detail will determine how our tapestries and relationships look. Lumpy? Uneven? Shot with gold and brilliant colors? God's pattern and instructions provide us with limitless possibilities. The question is: will we follow His perfect pattern?

IS THERE A PART TWO?

From the first half of this chapter, we have some ideas about improving what we weave, but because I am ever-practical, let's investigate how we can use them in our leadership roles.

HOW DO YOU HANDLE DIFFICULT PEOPLE?

I took a graduate course on dealing with difficult people! Isn't it amazing that we would have enough trouble with certain persons to warrant an entire class on how to build better relationships with them? The fifth chapter of this book will address conflict management, but it is important to realize how much our relationships can be affected by such individuals. When others try to manipulate, intimidate us, or work from hidden agendas, we must be intentional in our dealings with them and as well as with others who may be on the fringe of what is happening.

After you determine what is prompting a difficult person's behavior, you can take steps to deal individually with them. You can recognize inappropriate behavior by asking:

☒ Is their behavior immoral, illegal, or unethical?

☒ Are they trying to manipulate, which is a form of blackmail?

☒ Are their actions or behavior self-serving? Are they out to have their own way?

☒ Is their intent malicious? Is there verbal, emotional, or psychological abuse in their words or actions?

☒ Is the person out of control, showing rage or hysterical behavior?

☒ Is the person misusing her or his power and violating others' rights?

☒ Is the individual protecting "her" turf?

☒ Is the person determined to end up "on top?"

HOW DO WE MEND RELATIONSHIPS?

If we desire to be skilled leaders, it is essential to maintain relationships that are growing in positive directions and of benefit to all involved. Once personalities, background, and experiences enter the picture, it becomes apparent that coping skills will be necessary. There are many such skills we can adopt that will ensure that our relationships work.

If you can learn to do three things as a leader and in your personal relationships, you may increase your success in mending relationships that for one reason or another have been damaged or are toxic in nature. Here they are:

1. *Learn to solve problems.* Agree what the problem is; set a time to negotiate; remain calm; determine a deadline; realize that some things won't change; agree to be creative in solving the issue and open to new ideas; find resources as needed; restore the relationship.

2. *Learn to speak up.* This is especially necessary for leaders. We are wounded by family members, co-workers, friends, or our boss. Speaking up will help you minimize feelings of abandonment, rejection, guilt, anger, betrayal, and defensive thoughts.

3. *Learn to let go.* Remember what my friend said about correcting the holes in a woven piece? We must learn to let go of the embarrassing situations in our lives caused by a difficult person. Recall what happened, who was involved, the emotions you felt, and what was said. Then, let it go!

DOES STRESS AFFECT RELATIONSHIPS?

Of course it does! It challenges our relationships at home, work, school, church, and in our community. It hampers our ability to accurately "read" others' nonverbal communication, to utilize the coping skills we have, to recover from strong emotions, and even make sense of the world around us. Your responses to the questions below may give you an indication of how you are managing the stress in your life.

- When you are agitated, can you calm yourself quickly?
- Can you let go of your anger?
- Can you ask others to help you calm down and to feel better?
- When you get home at night, can you walk in feeling calm and relaxed?
- How often are you moody or distracted?
- Can you recognize when others seem upset?
- Do you turn to friends, co-workers, or family members to help you calm down?

You might be helped by a series of simple actions to relieve stress. Listening to music, stretching tense muscles, having calming scents around you, or letting a mint dissolve slowly in your mouth can help you regain your balance. Remember these the next time you face a tense leadership meeting! Our ability to regulate stress relates directly to the level of confidence with which we handle life's relationships.

RELATIONSHIPS AND TECHNOLOGY

There's that elephant again! I saw a cartoon that showed a man and woman standing on the sidewalk. She said to him, "This (relationship) isn't going to work. I'm looking for someone with more apps."

The student sits gazing at her computer, "I love my computer because all my friends are in it!"

Another cartoon showed a young man and woman, each with laptops, sitting at a bistro table. He looked at his screen and exclaimed, "Did you just break up with me?!"

How about the series of photos labeled, "The Day Einstein Feared Most"? Friends having coffee, all holding their phones, not looking at each other. A day at the beach with four friends on their phones. The date, where instead of looking at each other, the teen boy and girl stare at their cell phones. Enjoying the sites becomes a convertible ride with everyone but the driver looking at photos on their phones. The best photo showed a group of young adults out to eat and everyone at the table looking at their tablets, Kindles, and phones.

Perhaps Einstein was right to be fearful! Embracing today's technology, women's relationships have changed dramatically. Even a few months can make a difference in how technology is viewed.

Studies show that younger women prefer online shopping, tweeting, texting, chatting through social networking websites with fewer shopping trips to favorite discount department stores, bookstores, or major department stores. Do they miss loading their preschoolers into carts or wrestling with them through clothes racks? Not so much.

Do women fully engaged with technology miss the interaction with others? Not necessarily. They spend two or three minutes online and are caught up with friends. Two minutes after they post, they hear from 45 acquaintances and friends. These technological marvels are perfect for busy moms. My hairdresser says she saves hours because she can text back in under a minute, make and confirm appointments in a flash, and know where her kids are. Does she miss the ringing phone, snail mail, or even emails? Her response? "No!"

Linda Morgan shares facts on technology and relationships in an online article at ParentMap.com. In "Living Under (cyber) Cover? How Technology is Shaping Our Relationships," Morgan shares that a Pew Research Center study reports that people actually connect more when using the internet and mobile phones. "People's social worlds are enhanced by new communication technologies," wrote Pew study author, Keith Hampton. Women use technology to improve their family time by using shared calendars, Skype, Facebook, and other networks to stay in touch, and by using automatic bill paying features many businesses and agencies have.

By the Numbers

According to Pew Research Center statistics published in *Southern Indiana Business Source*, as of September 2013:

- 73 percent of adults online use social networking sites, including 69 percent of all men and 78 percent of all women.
- 71 percent use Facebook.
- 18 percent use Twitter.
- 17 percent use Instagram.
- 21 percent use Pinterest.
- 22 percent use LinkedIn.
- 90 percent of Internet users between the ages of 18 and 29 use social-networking sites, and 78 percent between the ages of 30 and 49.

THE GENERATIONAL DIVIDE

Unlike younger women, some women in their 40s and 50s assert that they miss the "face time" in their relationships and that they find getting together with friends is invaluable. Many state they feel as if people on Facebook really don't know who they are. That can't happen until you see someone. Can deep, loyal friendships develop from online interaction? Are Facebook relationships short-term and transient? For that matter, are they even real friendships? What happens to intergenerational wisdom and exchange of thoughts and ideas?

These are difficult questions to answer, aren't they? Each of us has her own perspective and, hopefully we have thought through how technology impacts us personally. That our work world, marriage and family life, and friendships are involved is obvious. How dependent we become on our smartphones, tablets, Kindles, laptops, Facebook, texting—ah, what a list! We may go back to what is expected of us. Expectations can be notoriously unrealistic. Simply because we hear our cell phones chirp with another text message, are we obligated to answer within two minutes? Because technology has revolutionized how we communicate, connect, shop, and do basic life tasks, women who didn't have these capabilities in decades past may have more trouble embracing them. They don't necessarily regard them as "marvels!"

THE OTHER SIDE OF THE COIN

In his article, "Technology's Impact on Social Relationships: The Data May Surprise You!," Tom Dellner wrote, "My relationships with technology and social media is a little like my relationship with fast food. I enjoy it immensely and find it semi-addictive, but deep down, I wonder what it's doing to me." He reported that Dr. Keith Hampton, communications professor at the University of Pennsylvania, reiterated the concerns people have about technology and relationships: people are becoming isolated, less diverse, less engaged in traditional social behaviors, and less intimate.

Surprisingly, Dellner's research did not substantiate these concerns. Technology is changing the nature of community and how our relationships are structured, but evidence doesn't support isolation, disengagement, or fewer social activities. Obviously, not all the data is in, nor have all the changes taken place, but our core networks are not decreasing. Surprisingly, more diversity and close relationships are reported by Internet and mobile device users.

This conflicting report caused me to wonder how women I know feel about technology in their lives and its impact on them. Women of different ages, various occupations, and lifestyles answered my six questions, and I've given their responses below. Answer the questions yourself as you read along!

TECHNOLOGY AND YOUR RELATIONSHIPS

1. Do you feel understood, known, and supported by other women, even if you aren't in the same room with then?
2. How important is face time to you?
3. What are your thoughts about talking on the phone or in person versus texting, Facebook, Twitter, instant messaging?
4. Do your relationships by way of social media lack depth and intimacy?
5. How have your friendships been affected by technology? Do you feel left behind?
6. Comment briefly about whether technology is a blessing or intrusion in your life.

As I read the responses to the six questions above, I learned two things. The opinions of those I surveyed about using technology were influenced by the women's age. How they felt about face-to-face interaction and the "intrusion versus blessing" aspects was markedly different. Younger women fell into the "embrace it" category while older women admitted, "they could take it or leave it a lot of the time."

One of the youngest women surveyed was evidently in the throes of an unnamed social media relationship drama. She asked me to clarify the question dealing with intrusion of technology. She responded with, "Oh, the word that comes to my mind is 'home-wrecker!'" She had experienced uncontrolled emotions by way of technology. In contrast with her feelings was the response of a retired woman who said technology wasn't an intrusion because she was in control and determined how much she used it and allowed it into her life.

Interesting, huh? The general response about technological abilities taking over was that because we can do all these things doesn't mean we have to let them dominate our time and responses. The second prominent attitude that surfaced was that those surveyed didn't think their personal relationships were being affected negatively. Again, older women stated they wouldn't allow technology to intervene and decrease interaction with friends and acquaintances. The speed with which they could communicate encouraged young women to maintain friendships and networks. The ability to do this quickly was seen as a huge benefit. Women who grew up without such capabilities still depend on the face-to-face interaction and felt there was no substitute for it.

On a side note, one woman wrote something I found extremely interesting: she loved texting and emailing because it allowed her to think about her responses before making them "actual." She admitted to being rather reserved and uncertain of what to say in person but that technology gave her the opportunity to check what she was saying. She likes using the backspace button on her computer and was definitely more comfortable with social media than interactions with others in person!

Granted my survey was a small one, but I saw both sides of the coin in the women's answers. Technology has changed the way we relate, yes. Technology provides us with many ways to stay in touch. How we manage what it brings into our lives is an individual choice. Technology can be controlled by the consumer!

TECHNOLOGY AND YOUR RELATIONSHIPS

1. Using Facebook, find and make contact with someone you knew in high school or college and have lost track of.
2. Keep a log for one week of how much time you spend on the Internet (for whatever reason).
3. For one week, record how much time you interact in person with others.
4. Choose a long-distance family member and communicate with them by way of texting, Instagram, or email.
5. Use Pinterest to find an unusual recipe and then post your opinion after making it.
6. If you haven't done very much Internet searching, look for new information about a hobby, purchase concert tickets,

or find facts about a new prescription your doctor has given you. No computer? Use one at the public library. Can you see how these activities directly or indirectly affect your relationships?

FIFTH AND SIXTH

Our society is characterized by diversity. When you work outside your home, or own an at-home business, plan a family reunion, have a block party, teach a Bible study, coordinate a support group, or head up the choir booster club at your son's school, you will be challenged by the diversity that meets you around every corner.

Relationships reflect the great diversity in our world. How do we as leaders deal with the diversity we meet every day and in all leadership associations? Here are several suggestions that may help you build relationships with people of different cultural backgrounds or relational values than your own.

- Learn about the person's culture (this can be experiential or value-oriented).
- If the diversity is experience-based, try to engage yourself in that culture. Expose yourself to the music, food, or traditions of another culture.
- Realize you will make mistakes.

We have seen other types of cultural change that can challenge us as leaders. Not all diversity trends may be viewed as positive. Faith Popcorn, CEO of Brain Reserve, reports:

- Single motherhood is no longer perceived as an unfortunate situation, but many times a conscious lifestyle decision.

- Today fewer US women in their early 30s are married than at any time since the 1950s.
- Because women have closed the financial gap, men are feeling negative side effects of the changing societal expectations.
- Alcoholism and suicide are on the rise among men as well as increases in the use of pornography.
- Women are purchasing weapons for protection, dispelling the notion that they need men to protect them.

All of these reported trends can influence relationships. As women marry, choose careers, and make leadership decisions, they will face these and other societal trends.

HOW DOES TECHNOLOGY AFFECT MY LEADERSHIP ROLES?

The danger posed to our leadership roles may come subtly as we gradually substitute electronic relationships for physical ones. A sense of isolation can result and we may find we are not connecting as effectively as we believe we are. This danger takes us back to the former discussion of effective communication. Texting "LOL" doesn't take the place of hearing real laughter. It is difficult to express real empathy electronically. We may tend to delay our response due to lack of the right words to "say."

In our leadership roles (committee chairpersons, supervisors, group leaders, community volunteers, or team leaders at church) there are several things to remember that will help us be more effective in our use of technology we have available to us.

☒ If you are uncomfortable saying something in-person, don't put it in an email or text.

☒ Even though you want to avoid replying, don't delay too long your response to messages.

☒ Remember online communication can dramatically affect your relationships.

☒ Balance time on the Internet with the time you spend physically with friends and family.

Relationships enrich our lives, but they can be messy. We are blessed because of the people we know and the connections we make, but those relationships can cause stress and become harmful. We learn, grow, and change through our relationships, but we may not always like the changes they bring. As our life tapestries are woven by our relationships, we need to be committed to using strong threads—God's will—as a foundation. With His strength, we will weather what those relationships bring into our lives.

THE ULTIMATE RELATIONSHIP

Our God is the One who comes to us, the great initiator of relationship. All of Scripture is the story of God's overtures to people. What we know of God is what God has chosen to reveal to us. In the Old Testament, we know about God through creation, mighty acts, personal contact with selected individuals, and through covenant promises, prophets, priests, and kings. The New Testament is the story of God made flesh—God with us. In the fullness of time, God's last and best Word appeared on the human landscape—Emmanuel. There is nothing more significant in all of history than the Cross and Resurrection events. It was God's gift to us of life, worth, blessing, and hope.

God invites us to be part of a relationship. "Behold, I stand at the door and knock. If anyone hears My voice and opens the door, I will come in to him and dine with him, and he with Me" (Revelation 3:20 NKJV). We are invited to be in relationship with God. We can have daily access to and fellowship with God. Through Christ we are restored into right relationship and are returned to the original blessing of creation.

The nature of the relationship between God and humankind is everlasting.

> *For I am persuaded that neither death nor life, nor angels nor principalities nor powers, nor things present nor things to come, nor height nor depth, nor any other created thing, shall be able to separate us from the love of God which is in Christ Jesus our Lord* (Romans 8:38–39 NKJV).

Our relationship with God is secure in Christ. Our God is faithful to the promises that we will not be forsaken. Fears come washing over us. We read the newspapers. We live in a violent and unsafe world. We seek safety. We are afraid of being alone. We seek comfort. We have suffered grievous loss. We have suffered betrayal from someone we thought was our friend. Loved ones die and leave us heartsore and stricken by shock and grief. Circumstances conspire to frighten us with the specter of poverty, illness, old age, and death. We cast about to find security. Where is there permanency in a world gone crazy? Only in Christ. This faithful God who comes to us and brings to us our rooting and our grounding, shows us, in Christ, how to live.

SEEING OURSELVES THROUGH GOD'S EYES

Why should God want to have a relationship with us? Have you ever made a quilt, painted a picture, or designed something? Do you remember the sense of accomplishment and pride you took in that simple act? Imagine how much more God takes pride in the created order. Imagine the pleasure God takes in having relationship with the crown of creation. We can begin to see ourselves, then, as God sees us: worthy and valuable.

It is at the point of our relationships one with another that our faith becomes practical. If faith has worth, it is lived out in our behavior. It is easy to think holy thoughts on Sunday morning but much more difficult to put those thoughts into loving actions Monday through Saturday. Scripture teaches us how to treat each other.

We can take the triune God as our definition of productive relationship. We can know how to relate to God and to each other. The thrust of Scripture deals with the ethical implications of our faith. It dictates the way we are to behave within our relationships. How can we say we love God if we don't love our neighbors, husbands, friends, or supervisors at work? One of the first Bible verses we teach children is, "Be kind to one another" (Ephesians 4:32 NKJV). Because God is love, we live in love and behave in loving ways.

(*Found Treasures: Finding Your Worth in Unexpected Places* is a fresh look at how women can develop a healthy self-esteem through studying God's Word, reflection, and stories about unusual "found" objects. Also available in digital format, it can be purchased online at: NewHopeDigital.com.)

The Weaver

My life is but a weaving
Between my Lord and me,
I cannot choose the colors
He worketh steadily.
Offtimes He weaveth sorrow,
And I in foolish pride
Forget He sees the upper
And I, the underside.
Not till the loom is silent
And the shuttles cease to fly
Shall God unroll the canvas
And explain the reason why.
The dark threads are as needful
In the Weaver's skillful hand
As the threads of gold and silver
In the pattern He has planned.

— AUTHOR UNKNOWN

3 TIME-MANAGEMENT ESSENTIALS

By Debbie Lloyd

"There is a time for everything, and a season for every activity under heaven."

ECCLESIASTES 3:1

LIFE IS LIKE A BOOKCASE

My son-in-law built floor-to-ceiling bookcases in my office for all the books I've collected. While the shelves are adjustable, they will only hold the books that fit in the width we decided would be adequate. If all of my new books are thin, I'm in good shape for several more years! However, that isn't working so well. Some of the shelves are already overflowing, and I've had to do some rearranging.

One night I heard a loud sound somewhere in the house. I turned over and went back to sleep thinking I would probably never know what it was. The next morning as I entered my office, I discovered the source of the sound. Two of the shelf holders had broken, spilling books all over the floor!

My life and the time I have in each day are like my office bookshelves. I have a tendency to force more and more into the same amount of time. Is your life anything similar to mine? Do you cram too much into the allotted time and then spend additional time cleaning up the resulting messes?

This chapter will deal with establishing priorities, how to deal with interruptions, learning to say no, and making conscious choices about your use of this precious commodity called time. Take a little time (it will be time well spent) to read the following pages. They *could* change your life!

THERE ISN'T ENOUGH TIME! OR IS THERE?

Please look up the following verses and see what the Bible says about time.

- Genesis 1:3–5; 14–15
- Psalm 74:16
- Matthew 25:29
- Ephesians 5:15–16
- Philippians 4:19
- Colossians 4:5

WHAT IS TIME MANAGEMENT?

Is it moving hurriedly through the day, checking off accomplished tasks from one's list? It must mean more than collapsing into bed at the end of a day holding a crumpled paper filled with affirming check marks . . . marks that chant, "Well done, Busy Bee! Look at all you did today!" Maybe that friend who called really needed more than the recipe. Perhaps the secretary in your office needed to talk to someone about her family's shaky financial situation after her uninsured 16-year-old's auto accident.

Time management is more than mechanically squeezing more activities into less time. I've always had the notion that busyness must be related to godliness. Actually, time management may be about doing less, for you see, time management is life management, discerning priorities, having the right perspective, claiming responsibility for our time, accepting interruptions as opportunities, learning when to delegate and when to say no, and feeling good about the choices we have made.

GOD IS FAIR

Each of us has 24 hours each day—no more, no less. Each hour is divided into 60 minutes, 3,600 seconds. The difference comes in what we do with our time. Another person may get more use out of her 3,600 seconds, but she gets not one second more. There is no way to put an extra hour here or an extra day there. We can, however, learn to make the best use of the time we have. When we master our time, we master our lives.

That is what Christian time management is all about. As we begin to listen for and abide by God's plan for our time, we learn to master it, not be mastered by it. The Apostle Paul said it well: "Be very careful, then, how you live—not as unwise but as wise, making the most of every opportunity, because the days are evil" (Ephesians 5:15–16).

God gives us time and it belongs to Him, as our money, talents, and children do. If we acknowledge God's ownership of time, we must also acknowledge that He can stretch it to fit our needs. God will supply all our needs (Philippians 4:19), including time. God doesn't give us a greater number of minutes, but instead helps us use the minutes more efficiently. He increases the quality of what we produce in the amount of time we have.

The Lord's instruction about being a good steward applies to our use of time as well. Paul instructed the early church to "make the best possible use of your time" (Colossians 4:5 Phillips). The Ephesians were charged to use their time wisely and to "make the most of every opportunity you have for doing good" (Ephesians 5:16 TLB). We will also be asked to account for how we spent our time as the servants in Jesus' parable (Matthew 25:29 TLB).

⚜ PROFILE OF THE MASTER MANAGER ⚜

We would be negligent if we did not look at the life of Jesus for some hint as to how to better organize our time. All four Gospel writers present a picture of Jesus under constant pressure, being pursued by friends and enemies, acquaintances and strangers. His every word was monitored, every gesture commented on, every action analyzed. Even so, I never get the feeling that He was rushed, that He had to play "catch up," or that He was taken by surprise. His life showed a wonderful balance, a holy sense of time.

Why was Jesus able to control His time? In Ordering Your Private World, *Gordon MacDonald notes three reasons why Jesus commanded control of His time.*

1. He understood His mission. *With a key task to perform, He measured His use of time against that sense of mission. Because He had a clear vision of His mission, not even Satan could convince Him to shortcut His Father's eternal priorities.*

2. Jesus understood His own limitations and knew the source of His power. *Jesus realized that properly budgeting His*

time would compensate for human weaknesses when spiritual warfare began. Private time, such as the 40 days in the wilderness and the prayer in Gethsemane, were a fixed item on Jesus' time budget. He not only knew His limits; He also knew the source of His strength.

3. Jesus made intentional choices about His time. *He invested prime time, taking the disciples through the Scriptures, explaining the deeper meaning of His messages to the crowds. Valuable hours were seized in order to debrief them when they returned from assignments, to rebuke them when they failed, and to affirm them when they succeeded. Jesus practiced the principle: where your priorities are, there your time will be.*

THERE IS ENOUGH TIME!

Jesus was never caught short of time. He knew His mission; He was spiritually sharpened by moments alone with God; and He used wisdom when choosing the focus of His time and energy. At the end of three short years of ministry, He was able to say, "I have finished the work which thou gavest me to do" (John 17:4 KJV). He really is the Master Manager!

To command control of our time we must discover our own purpose as followers of Christ and must establish priorities in line with this purpose. As Jesus was spiritually sharpened by moments alone with God, we, too, must budget time for instruction and guidance from the Lord.

FIRST THINGS FIRST

"But seek first his kingdom and his righteousness, and all these things will be given to you as well" (Matthew 6:33). Seek the kingdom first. In order to gain control of our time, we must clearly understand our mission and measure our use of time against that understanding. To budget our time more effectively, we must first establish priorities within the framework of our life's calling, then set concrete goals to help us live in keeping with those priorities.

One of the first steps in becoming a better life manager is to have a clear sense of purpose. What are we to be about as people of God? We are to be His witnesses, to share His love with those about us.

As Christ followers we quickly claim "Seek first the kingdom of God" (Matthew 6:33) as a directive for living. But what does this mean? Some may be guided by the thinking, "God first, others second, myself last." We cannot, however, put our lives in compartments. We're not to serve Jesus first, then family, then church, and on down a list. Rather, we are to serve Jesus *as* we serve our family, church, work, community, and our own needs.

This thinking affirms that everything I do is important to God. He is concerned about, and seeks to be a part of, every aspect of my life. This truth relieves much of my guilt about not spending enough time on spiritual things. My personal devotional life and efforts to know God more intimately are vital and deserve deliberate planning. I must seek God all during the day. I must begin my day asking, "How can I seek the kingdom of God today?" and let that question carry me all through the day.

In *The Gift of Time*, William T. McConnell gave a fresh understanding of these instructions from the Lord. McConnell concluded that seeking the kingdom is a basic attitude that defines a Christian's priorities. Consider your use of time and determine if seeking the kingdom is a priority for you.

1. **To know God**

   Seeking first the kingdom of God implies the need to set aside time to get to know God, His ways, and His desires. Imagine the relationship that would result from a husband and wife who shared a general commitment but never saw or talked to one another. As seekers after God, we must plan into our days: times to read and study the Bible, pray, and worship.

2. **To take on His character**

   It is only as we spend time with the Lord that we begin to take on His likeness. What an awesome adventure—to be like Jesus.

3. **To serve Him**

   As we become committed to taking on Christ's character, we will naturally seek to serve Him, follow His teachings, and obey His commands—love others, seek justice, work toward harmony in our world, minister to those in need. This service would include those closest to us, our extended family, those in our Christian community, and the needy in general.

4. **To represent Him in every aspect of our life**

   We are called to represent Christ, to be His spokespersons, to be His incarnation, to continue His work. We are to be bridge builders, connecting others to Him.

5. **To bring others to Him**

   The logical outgrowth of building bridges that connect individuals to God's redemptive love is the growth of the kingdom. This is evangelism . . . providing an opportunity for others to experience the redemptive love of God. Jesus instructed, "As you go, make disciples." While you are about your daily tasks, share the good news. This is lifestyle evangelism.

WHAT ABOUT YOU?

Read Luke 18. How does Jesus illustrate the importance of focusing on priorities?

1. What do you consider your number one mission in life?

2. What are some other things that God has called you to do?

3. In what way do (or should) these priorities influence your time schedule?

❧ ADDING HOURS TO YOUR DAY ❧

"Reverence for God adds hours to each day" (Proverbs 10:27 TLB). The Master Manager not only knew His purpose and mission in life. By His example He taught us the importance of regularly spending time seeking direction and gathering strength to accomplish that mission. Luke's account of Mary and Martha

provides a vivid lesson of how we should spend our time. Like Martha, I seem to be so focused on doing good things to please God that I don't take the time for the best, to hear Him, to learn from Him, and to enjoy His presence in my life.

While time management experts may suggest we be like Martha and get more done in less time, Jesus said it was Mary who chose the good thing. When we choose to sit at Jesus' feet, the Martha-tasks more easily fall into place. It is in the daily process of taking the time to sit at the Lord's feet, and in regularly taking time off, that we identify and gain the power to live out our priorities.

TAKING TIME TO SIT AT THE LORD'S FEET

In my daily devotional time I jumped from one method to another, trying to find the right one for me. I was easily distracted from the task by interruptions and other responsibilities. I also felt guilty when, in my busyness, my quiet time would wane into a time of planning, list making, and organizing my day. Somehow, even through the guilt, the activity seemed to have sort of a sacred effect when first thing in the morning I thought over my day and made lists, schedules, and agendas, and then prayed about the tasks of the day. I knew it wasn't what all the books said to do in a quiet time, but part of it felt right.

While preparing to write this chapter, I had one of those "aha" experiences as I read William McConnell's *The Gift of Time* (now out of print). The author read my mind and expressed my own frustration with my personal quiet time!

The author explains that when we read a prepared devotion or a few verses of Scripture out of context, our quiet time is isolated from the concerns of our normal daily activities. He suggests that we make our devotional time more connected with our everyday life. If our personal planning and time management includes space for a quiet time, why shouldn't our quiet time contribute to our planning or time management?

McConnell suggests that if we included a time for planning in our quiet time, we could orient our entire day toward God instead of trying to find a few moments here and there to squeeze Him in. By including planning as a part of our quiet time, four things happen:

1. Our devotions are not separated from the rest of our activities.
2. Our planning can be done in the context of prayer and God's Word.
3. We affirm our commitment to the purpose and values of the kingdom of God.
4. We experience the guidance of the Holy Spirit in establishing our priorities and plans.

TIMELY QUESTIONS

- After choosing a Scripture passage (using a devotional book, missions periodical, or prayer guide), read it several times.
- Ask yourself questions that focus your attention on your relationship with God, through thanksgiving and confession. *What am I grateful for? What in the text leads me to thanksgiving? What do I need to confess concerning this text?*
- Ask questions that deal with your response to God in your daily life through intercession and obedience. *How should this passage impact how I pray? What does the Lord require of me here?*

- Ask questions that link your quiet time to how you plan the use of the rest of your time. *What should I do? What should I not do?*

Using this process, our daily to-do list will come out of our time with God. As Ananias was instructed to visit Saul (Acts 9:10–19), we may be led to include in our plans things we might have otherwise known nothing about or certainly avoided if we had known. We must remember how different God's ideas of managing the kingdom are from ours. Many times we confuse our own interests with what we think God wants us to do.

Because most of our time is concerned with normal day-to-day responsibilities (families, work, church, civic duties, and so on), thoughts about these "things to do" often intrude into our quiet time. Instead of trying to dismiss these thoughts as worldly concerns, sent from the devil to disrupt your spiritual devotion, McConnell suggests that we write them down. This frees our minds of them and also helps us determine our priorities. In praying about each of these responsibilities, we can get a clearer idea of how each contributes to the kingdom of God.

ABOUT THAT TIME ALONE

Asking questions about our quiet time provides an opportunity to evaluate our use of the time. Why didn't I do what was on my list for yesterday? You may discover you simply had too much to do, or you underestimated how much time a certain activity would take. You may have added activities others could have done, things you thought others expected of you, or things you included, hoping God would approve. Your quiet time may also show you that you need to say no more often!

MAKE THE TIME

- If you are not already committed to a daily devotional time, what steps do you need to take to make this a priority?
- How can you incorporate your daily planning into your time at the Lord's feet?

THE GOOD NEWS AND THE BAD NEWS

Here it is: there's good news about time management! And, there's bad news about time management. If you believe that change can happen, the good news is that you can take control of the demands on your time. The bad news is that you will have to initiate the changes that need to take place before you can control your time.

Leader and author John Maxwell said, "You will never change your life until you change what you do daily. The secret of your success is found in your daily routine." If we refuse to acknowledge that we should reorganize our time, we will never reach the place where we control time, rather than having it control us.

If the good news is that you can take control of your time and manage it efficiently, what steps can you take to *be* an effective time manager? *Be* realistic regarding what is possible. *Be* attentive to your goals and dreams. *Be* confident that you can make life better. *Be* alert and stop things before they spiral out of control. *Be* diligent in returning things to their places and in order.

WHAT THINGS CAUSE YOU TROUBLE REGARDING TIME?

You may...

- be easily distracted and can't stick to one thing.
- move more slowly than others. Keep going in the right direction and stay focused.
- not be knowledgeable about time management. These skills can be learned.
- simply be overwhelmed and feel as if you are drowning.
- let your creativity get in the way because you are more interested in trying new things than in finishing the jobs you already have begun.
- have others with whom you work who create problems for you that take large blocks of time that you had allocated for doing other things.

WHAT ABOUT YOU?

Which of these areas in your life are not under control?

☐ Family life
☐ Other relationships
☐ Career
☐ Education
☐ Health
☐ House

What do you do well already?

☐ organized activities

☐ housework
☐ correspondence
☐ storage systems

List three areas where you need to improve.

Do you cram too much into the time you have?

What hinders you the most in using your time effectively?

Are you willing to make some changes in how you use your time?

SETTING GOALS FOR MANAGING YOUR TIME

Did you think goals were only for other areas of life? Stop and think now. Once we have acknowledged our purpose, it is important to set goals—to have a plan for life and a strategy of attack. There is nothing like trying to get somewhere without directions; what a real waste of time! "In his heart a man plans his course, but the LORD determines his steps" (Proverbs 16:9).

We get up in the morning, go through the motions, stay very busy, even get tired, but at the end of the day we look back and ask, "What did I accomplish?" We often accomplish so little and waste so much time because we do not know where we are going.

Goals = Direction

The first step in fulfilling our God-given purpose is to establish some directions by setting some precise goals. When it comes to being better managers of our time, goals are essential. As seekers of the kingdom, we all need specific goals to guide us in the use of our time. Why do goals keep us from wasting time?

1. **Goals are motivators.** Goals motivate us to take action. Like roadside mile markers, they allow us to see how far we have come and how far we need to go. Goals keep us from wasting time by helping us know what to do next.

2. **Goals are tools for decision-making.** Goals help us make decisions based not on immediate emotions but rather on sound judgment. Read the account of when Lazarus was ill and how Jesus responded by thoughtfully continuing in His ongoing task and then going to Bethany.

   It has been said that the important things in life are seldom urgent, and the urgent things are seldom important. The account of Mary and Martha verifies that claim. Martha became a victim of false urgency as she prepared a meal for the Lord while her sister, Mary, focused on the important matter of sitting with the Lord. Often we become victims of the urgent rather than doers of the important.

3. **Goals are tools for measuring progress.** Goals keep us from wasting time by showing us how far we've come.

When there is nothing by which to measure our progress, our time will disappear as mysteriously as money in a poorly managed bank account.

4. **Goals are stress reducers.** We can see that stress and the achievement of goals are closely related. Focusing on the accomplishments rather than the time involved may reduce stress. By concentrating our efforts toward meeting certain goals, we find personal guidelines and direction, and we can reduce much of the stress of doing, doing, doing.

MORE ABOUT GOAL SETTING

It is important to set both long- and short-range goals. By setting and reaching manageable short-range goals, long-range goals become attainable. Goals should include several basic characteristics:

- **Worthwhile.**
- **Specific and measurable** (for example, to lose ten pounds by next year).
- **Attainable**—not so low that they offer no challenge (to lose a pound), but not so high as to be discouraging (to look like Miss America by next week).
- **Flexible.** Remember, circumstances change and priorities shift. Don't fail to be sensitive to the need to alter your personal goals.
- **Written.** This helps you visualize your objectives, strengthen your commitment, and provide a basis for reviewing and checking your progress.

WHAT ABOUT YOU?

Take time to set some goals for your life, both long-range and short-range in the following areas. Keep in mind that goal setting should be specific, measurable, attainable, scheduled, and flexible.

Physical

Spiritual

Financial

Personal

Relational

Educational

Occupational

Social

LAST THOUGHTS ABOUT GOALS

Commit your goals to prayer. Share them with a close friend or your spouse. Mull over them and return to them in several days to revise and polish them. Take note of the benefits of achieving these goals and some of the obstacles you will face in pursuing them. Think about what you need to help you realize these goals. Then, use these goals as the Master Manager did—to help provide direction and structure as you move toward organization of your life and your time.

A PERSONAL RETREAT

On several occasions, Jesus withdrew from the crowd, retreating from the busyness of life. Scripture depicts Jesus retreating after busy, people-filled occasions. He knew the value of time alone to regroup, rethink, reevaluate, and refuel. It is also interesting to note that the times after this solitude were always filled with power and the miraculous—Jesus walked on water, calmed the storm, healed a paralytic.

We, too, need time in the mountains. Group worship, private devotional time, and regular Bible study are essential, but sometimes larger chunks of time are necessary to keep from getting bogged down in the details of daily living. A personal retreat gives time to look at the whole picture of one's life and to seek direction from God. Make the effort to set aside retreat time even though it may be very difficult. Schedule it whenever you can. If you cannot set aside the time monthly, consider retreating every other month or quarterly.

Write the date on your calendar, and when the time comes, gather your Bible, hymnal, calendar, notebook, and pen—and leave home. One busy woman insists that leaving home is a must because at home there are too many distractions, such as the telephone and seeing work that needs to be done.

Choose a spot such as the library, a park, the beach, or even your parked car for your retreat. Include these things in your retreat time:

- Find a specific Scripture that you can claim as a promise for the next month.
- Sing or read hymns. There is wonderful doctrine to be found in them!
- Plan the coming month in as much detail as possible—noting personal, children's, spouse's, and family's commitments that concern you. Take stock of wardrobe needs, meal planning, and household and cleaning projects. Try to nail down specific dates whenever possible.
- Bathe all your plans with prayer.

One of the most productive times of my life was the time I spent in the mountains on a personal retreat. Granted, I was there at the children's camp as the Missionary of the Week, but aside from a daily 30-minute presentation, my time was my own. I decided I would spend my leisure time in retreat. I took devotional materials, my Bible, my calendar, and a binder with my to-do list. Those five days were wonderful and created a master plan for personal and professional work. It was one of my best years because of the time away!

DID YOU SAY "TAKE TIME OFF"?!

The word *leisure* comes from the Latin, *licere*, meaning "to be permitted." We need to give ourselves permission to relax. We would do well to imitate Jesus' example. Following the sixth day of creation, God deliberately stopped working. He took time to relax. No, He wasn't tired. I'm sure He didn't need to recuperate. God set aside time to enjoy His creation. Even with biblical examples to verify the importance of leisure, we still often feel guilty when we take the time to relax.

In her book, *Overwhelmed*, author Brigid Schulte discusses her struggles to carve out leisure time. She describes her life as being "scattered, fragmented, and exhausting." In a *Redbook* magazine article adapted from Schulte's book, she tells how she called John Robinson, Oxford University research associate and time guru, who has studied how typical people spend their time doing on typical days.

She expressed her concern that women are too tired to even read the newspaper. Surprisingly, Robinson did not agree with her assessment. He asserts that women have 30 hours of leisure time every week and demonstrated his statement by going through her weekly schedule. He circled running as leisure; visiting a friend in the hospital as leisure; listening to the radio as leisure; and talking on the phone to a friend while taking her son's bike to be repaired as leisure.

Schulte's response? "They didn't feel very leisurely!" She believes that *how* we feel about an activity matters more than *what* we are doing. Other studies indicate that we have convinced ourselves that extreme busyness is a virtue. Americans work longer days and have the least vacation time of any country. Do we feel compelled to be busy? Have we come to believe that we are leading worthy lives if we are busy to the extreme?

Ellen Galinsky, president of the Families and Work Institute, another research organization, quoted in the *Redbook* article, says "For women, the to-do list is always going and . . . having the tape running in your head about it all the time." Research has found that women feel they must *earn* leisure rather than they *deserve* it. The mental-tape that runs through many women's minds is called "contaminated time." Even when they are having fun, on the inside they are processing what is still on their list.

Did you know that our working memory can keep only about seven things in it at a time? Schulte encourages women to clear the clutter in their minds and to choose a few priorities for their focus that week. Having a clearer idea of what is important and what is urgent will help a woman utilize her time wisely, minus the sense of foreboding that undermines productivity and enjoyment of the activity.

We need to think of leisure time as something we do for God's purpose. Instead of thinking that we work in order to have leisure time, it is more appropriate to realize that we spend time in leisure in order to get on with our work. Modern industry has learned the value of time away from work, thus coffee breaks and mandatory vacations.

Now hear this! We *must* assume responsibility for our leisure time! Yes . . . read that again. We *must* assume responsibility for our leisure time. Rarely will someone else insist that we take it.

Sadly, many find that planning for leisure is often more difficult than planning work. Personally, if I wait until all my work is done before I sit down to sew (one of my leisurely treats), I grow more and more frustrated because my list never gets completed and I never make it to the sewing machine.

Leisure means different things to different people. My husband enjoys mowing the yard. For me, that is forced labor. My friend Sharon will sit for hours, relaxing with a good book. Leisure for some means going to a movie, entertaining guests, baking bread, going for a walk. Give *me* half an hour for a refreshing bicycle ride or a dip in the pool!

Sometimes it is best to take leisure as it comes, packaged in various sizes and shapes. It may be an occasional weekend retreat or getaway with a friend, a date with your spouse, or a bubble bath after the children are finally in bed. Leisure, like gifts, sometimes comes in surprise packages to be ripped into and enjoyed impulsively.

Taking time off for leisure does not mean taking time off from God's plan for our life. Rather, it is refreshing ourselves for the work He has for us to do. We must learn to follow the example of the Master Manager, who regularly took time to pray, to plan, and even to relax. It is in taking the time for a daily quiet time, periodic getaways for planning and renewal, and regular time off for leisure and relaxation that we find the needed direction and strength for the journey ahead.

What About You?

1. List some activities you like to do to relax.
2. Look at your weekly schedule and circle the leisure time you have.

3. If you have had a personal retreat, plan another. If not, set aside time when you can look at your priorities, set goals, and enjoy God's blessings of family, friends, and life.

> *"Women's lives have never been more complex, multi-faceted and demanding than they are today."*
>
> SHE MEANS BUSINESS, BY GRANT SCHNEIDER

IT'S ALL ABOUT CHOICES

Every woman makes choices. Regardless of her various roles and responsibilities, she is able to decide her priorities. Let's look at some of the ways she spends her time.

CONFESSIONS

Confessions of a Volunteer Leader

I am committed to ministries and activities that use the training and interests I have. My commitment to be active means I'm not always available to take care of my grandchildren or leave on an unplanned getaway. I believe God is using me to create community awareness about children living in poverty.

Confessions of a Single Parent

I didn't choose to be a single parent, but I am trying to do my best. I am employed outside my home and spend evenings with my children, doing housework, and trying to make it financially. I've chosen to be at home at night rather than attending committee meetings at church. I limit my weekend activities so housework and homework are finished in readiness for the new week.

Confessions of a Stay-at-Home Mom

Because I have chosen marriage and a family, I can accept that keeping the house clean is part of my responsibility. I still have choices though! I choose how that work is done, when it's done, and how I can be involved in my community and church. I choose to limit extra-curricular activities and carpooling so my time isn't splintered so much of the time.

Confessions of a Retirement Rebel

I'm not "hangin' around." I've become involved in several projects in my community as a volunteer counselor. I love working with women who have made difficult decisions regarding their unexpected pregnancies. My activities mean my house isn't always clean, and I don't always have nutritious meals, but the choices are mine.

Confessions of a Working Woman

I know all women work! But, I have to work outside my home and spend many hours away from my family. I'd rather be home, but I can't do that right now so I've made some choices to not accept extra projects even though there would be more pay. I limit working overtime, and take no more than one overnight business trip a month.

DON'T SKILLS COUNT?

Time-management skills are not the first step to putting order in our lives. First, we must recognize that time is a gift from God, and that His priorities can always be fulfilled in the amount of time we have been given. Doing God's will does not mean meeting every request that school, church, work, or civic groups propose. Instead, it means knowing what God has and has not called us to do.

Remember: the choice is yours! Once you have made prayerful decisions about your time, accept with confidence the choices you have made and begin to take control of your time. Take the time to evaluate those choices periodically. Realize that your choices will not necessarily be the same as someone else's. There is no need to feel guilty because others have chosen differently. Be willing to accept the decisions that others have made about their time.

Because you are the master of your time and must answer to God for its wise use, it is up to you to take responsibility for the choices you make. You must continually sort through the opportunities available to you and sift out those that do not fit into the life-plan God has shown you. When faced with an overwhelming number of obligations and a limited amount of time, stop and ask yourself, "Is time the problem, or am I the problem?" Then do something about it!

Managing your time is important, but you will never manage your time until you learn to manage yourself.

WALK WISELY

> *Be very careful, then, how you live—not as unwise, but as wise, making the most of every opportunity because the days are evil* (Ephesians 5:15–16).

Part of determining if you are using your time wisely might be in your answers to these questions. Your answers may reveal what areas of time management need your attention and skill development.

- Do you have trouble deciding what to do first?
- Do you ever forget where you are in a project?
- Is setting priorities easy or hard for you?
- Is your life controlled by the needs of others?

FIND TIME, TAKE TIME, MAKE TIME

We must learn how to invest our time to receive the greatest possible return for the minutes and hours God has given us. We've been talking about choices. The choices you make regarding how you use your time are some of the most important ones you'll make! And, they will require self-discipline!

The next few pages are going to guide you into thinking about your schedule, your time management techniques, principles of time management, and how you as a leader can maximize the time you have to accomplish the most. Speaking of schedules, the French word for "route" means a "well-traveled road." All of us need a schedule for doing the humdrum, ordinary, predictable things that happen on a regular basis.

Scheduling activities, projects, or meetings efficiently can make a world of difference in our lives. It can be the difference between a "horrible, terrible, no good, very bad day," as psychoanalyst and author Judith Viorst characterizes in her famous children's story, and one that leaves us with a sense of accomplishment and well-being.

Here are some suggestions you might find helpful as you schedule your days at work, home, church, or with others as a leader.

- Decide in advance how you will handle certain things to save time when they happen.
- Make it a matter of routine to schedule certain types of appointments or activities on certain days.
- Develop a system of dealing with mail, email messages, texts, and so on: Handle a message once. Don't pick it up, set it aside, and pick it up again later.
- Set a specific time to handle specific things (mail, telephone calls, and so on).

Take advantage of tools available to you. My daughter does the majority of her teaching administrative duties on her iPad. I don't think I've seen her with sticky notes in years! Smartphones, iPads, notebooks, tablets. . . . all have apps that can store info, provide reminders that will keep you organized and scheduled. This part of our technologically invaded lives is a very real plus!

Other time-management techniques can work for you. Go into any bookstore, and you will find many books on time management that purport to be "the answer" to all your time-related problems. Choosing one that fits you might take a lot of time! However, here are several techniques that might help you become more efficient in your use of time.

- **Approach #1:** Make a list of what you have to do on Monday. Then group the first two and out to the side write which of the two is the most important. Go through the rest of the list, doing the same thing. If your list has 12 things on it, you'll now have 6 that you've decided are the most important. Group the remaining 6 into 2s and so on until you have one item remaining on the list. This is similar to playing a series of tennis games, similar to a round-robin. Short, easy and it could work for you!

- **Approach #2:** Take a piece of paper and divide it into fourths. Label the four squares: Urgent & Important (i.e. not optional); Not Urgent but Important (i.e. the powerful things on your list that are easy to ignore but make life better if you'll do them); Urgent but Not Important (have a degree of urgency that makes you respond); and Not Urgent & Not Important (use these as breaks from the tension of urgent and important things on your list).

- **Approach #3:** Prioritize your to-do list by assigning each A, B, or C. A absolutely must get done. B had better be done. C could be done or you can let it slide.

WHAT ABOUT YOU?

Practice planning and prioritizing. Make a list of ten things you must do today. Prioritize your list using the ABC system. Now, try inserting these tasks into an actual schedule.

TIMELY NOTE

Not every activity in your day has the same value. You realize that, right? You've read about the "urgent" and the "important." Finding your son's gym shorts may be urgent to him, but that's probably not as important as signing your daughter's permission form to attend the Shakespearean play, which will determine 25 percent of her semester grade.

There's a wooden plaque in a friend's kitchen that reads, "Lack of preparation on your part does not necessarily constitute an emergency on my part." What week goes by in your life that you don't have the urgent taking precedence over the important?

- Nonessential items crowd into the date book long before the necessities.
- The most important things never seem to scream out when ignored.
- When we neglect our spiritual disciplines, God does not shout loudly about it.
- When we do not allocate time for family, they are generally understanding and forgiving. If they are neglected too long (when family, rest, and spiritual disciplines are finally noticed), it is often too late to avoid adverse consequences.

You will "find" a great deal of time by carefully planning whatever you really want to do.

Like the Master Manager, the busiest people find the time to do what they want to do not because they have any more time than others, but because they think in terms of "making" time by carefully planning, prioritizing, and scheduling.

Now that you have some techniques in your toolbox, use the following principles to use your time more efficiently.

Principle #1: Getting started.

For this step, using the A, B, C approach might help you in the beginning. You can always move to your own system as you become more accustomed to using the techniques. Review your list at the end of the day or the beginning of the next. Add what needs to be added from the old to the new to-do list, and omit those items that can be left undone. Some of yesterday's Bs may have become today's As, but also some became today's Cs or can be omitted entirely. Prioritize the new list and begin again, finding satisfaction in completing those priority tasks.

Still reluctant to get started? Don't be tempted to turn to a few easy Cs, telling yourself that you need a larger block of time for the As. The problem is, those large blocks of uninterrupted time seldom arise. So go on and start on an A task even if you have to spread the task over several small blocks of time.

Take your prioritized to-do list and start assigning them to time slots. Group similar items together, such as errands, phone calls, or correspondence.

Be realistic when you begin to schedule your list. Allow enough time to accomplish each task, but build in "slack time"—a quarter to a third of your day—for unplanned demands on your time. Allow even more than that if you have small children. Don't try to schedule yourself too optimistically or you'll end up feeling frustrated.

Principle #2: Plan and budget your time.

When I take the time to plan, I find I have more time. When I stop to think ahead about what needs to be done, I approach the day in a more orderly manner. Planning can improve the quality of life, give a sense of direction, and provide a feeling of accomplishment. It develops self-confidence and confirms and strengthens priorities. Surprisingly, planning helps us to be more flexible.

There are advantages to planning in the morning, when you are fresh. With the day's priorities clearly in mind, you are less likely to be sidetracked as you go along. Some prefer planning in the evening. Reflecting on what they have done that day helps them select what needs to be done tomorrow. Most of us learned to budget money years ago. When money is limited, we must budget. When time is in limited supply, the same principle holds true. Budgeting your time means determining ahead of time how your time is going to be allotted.

Principle #3: Weekly schedules may help.

The key in laying out a weekly schedule is to block out time for those big tasks, tough jobs, or goal-oriented projects. Reserve particular days of the week, such as Tuesday and Thursday mornings, for major projects. Start small by allocating 15 minutes a day to use exclusively for important items.

Try blocking A time (for those A items) horizontally on a weekly calendar—at the same time each day, Monday through Friday. In "finding" time to write this chapter, I discovered that it was too easy to find other activities to do. At the end of each day I would say, "Gee I just didn't have much time to write today." So in order to complete the task I had to block out time. I was finally learning that old planning principle: there is always enough time for those things that are important to you.

Besides daily planning, take time at the end of the week to review the week's progress and make general plans for the week to come. My husband and I use Sunday afternoon as planning time. We both spend some time alone, and then we get together to compare calendars, discuss transportation, home and car maintenance, and shopping needs for the week, and negotiate family time.

Principle #4: Personalize a system.

Once you review all the different approaches, don't take too long determining which one will work best for you. There are numerous systems you can use for scheduling—cell phone apps, day planners, iPads, desk or wall calendars. The apps on our phones are wonderful for hour-by-hour appointments or reminders. Computer-designed calendars can be emailed to your boss, co-workers or family. Any of these systems will do four things for you:

1. Provide balance between short- and long-range planning.
2. Provide a record of what has been done as well as what needs to be done.
3. Be accessible to others (family, spouse, work associates) who have need to know what your future commitments are.
4. Be a simple, habit-forming system that does not take too much time to prepare, maintain, or use.

STEP BACK AND LOOK AT HOW YOU MANAGE TIME AS A LEADER

Does all of this talk about time management have anything to do with our leadership lives? Absolutely! If you are not organized to manage your personal time, you won't be doing it in your leadership roles either. Do you have trouble deciding what to do first? Is it difficult for you to prioritize your tasks? Does having choices confuse you?

If you answered yes to any of these questions, you may need to develop a plan or system for organizing the responsibilities you have as a leader. This is essential no matter what type of leadership roles you have. If you lead a support group, your will need to decide the group's priorities. If you lead a women's Bible study, it will require you to organize your study materials. Serving as a volunteer at an annual community social services event means you will have to make some choices regarding finances, schedules, and activities.

One of the best experiences I've ever had was when I was asked to take on a key regional leadership position with a group of churches that wanted to provide missions experiences for women. I was required to submit a detailed plan of how we would use funds allocated to us an entire year in advance. It was quite a project! Each event or activity needed a separate worksheet outlining its purpose, persons responsible for details, and costs involved. It forced our team to organize, plan, and put into action our goals for the year. This laid the groundwork for many projects in the future, and I'm forever grateful for the experience.

Note: There are many types of planning sheets you can use to help you manage large projects and budgets. If you aren't required to use a specific one at work or church, search online for samples.

The effective leader needs three things to be an effective manager of her time:

- ☒ *The correct systems:* choose the system that helps you the most and matches your work ethic and personality the best.

- ☒ *The correct tools:* remember our discussion about using smartphones, iPads, tablets, and so on to your advantage? Make them work for you!

- ☒ *The correct habits:* This is critical for your success. Clutter is not your friend! If you work at home, the same rules apply. Put things away when you are finished with them. Have specific places for everything. This applies to your storage, filing cabinet, desk drawers, or the shelves in your office closet.

Habits and routines can make a difference in your efficiency. Once you have decided which system to use and what tools are available to you, the value of correct habits can't be underestimated. Ritual is important to managing our time. The ritual needs to be simple enough to do every day. It needs to be clear enough to keep you focused, and efficient enough to not get in your way. Last, it needs to be comprehensive enough to include what works and what doesn't.

WHAT ABOUT ME? I WORK FROM HOME

Answer these questions about your home workspace and environment.

1. Do you have a system for dealing with clutter in your workspace?
2. What is your strategy for dealing with interruptions during your work hours?
3. How have you communicated with your family about their demands on your time?
4. How would you rate your focus on work tasks?

THE MASTER MANAGER

Overcommitment is a major time waster. Recall Jesus' words to Martha: "You are worried and upset about many things, but only one thing is needed" (Luke 10:41–42). Jesus reminded us of the danger of trying to do too much. He personally made use of tools for battling overcommitment, including separating the urgent from the important, saying no, and delegating.

Jesus was able to tell the difference between the urgent and the important. When He was told He must go to Bethany because Lazarus was dying, He knew it was more important to continue His present task and go to Bethany later. He discerned the Father's will day by day in a life of prayer, thus warding off the urgent and accomplishing the important. This gave Him a sense of direction, set a steady pace, and enabled Him to do every task God had assigned.

We live in constant tension between the urgent and the important and are often tempted to let urgent tasks crowd out the most important. Calling for instant action, these demands seem to pressure every hour of every day. We can all recall Christmases where we spent so much energy in preparation that when the day finally arrived we were too exhausted to enjoy it. What teacher hasn't experienced days when she was so involved in the demands of the day that the needs of individual children went unnoticed?

The problem is that the important tasks (prayertime, quality time with my children, a date with my husband, a conversation with that non-Christian friend) rarely call out as loudly as the urgent. Because they can more easily be neglected, we often do not notice the results until it is too late.

How can we decide in our own lives what is important and what is urgent?

☒ Seek God's guidance as Jesus did.

☒ Pray for the Lord's direction and wait for His instructions.

☒ Reflect on your priorities.

☒ Get an overview picture of how you spend your time by making a personal time inventory.

☒ Ask yourself, "Will it matter five years from now?"

When faced with a decision about how to spend our time, we

must use Christ as our example and separate the important from the urgent.

THE HURRIER I GO

Although we develop strategies to manage our time, there are outside forces at work against us. Learning when to say "no" instead of agreeing to do everything is a problem for most women. Failure to delegate undermines our best intentions. You have your day and week planned and along comes a series of interruptions. Is there anything you can do about them? And then there's procrastination! Let's take the time (hmmm) and evaluate how each of these areas impacts the daily management of our time.

Break the Yes Habit

Many lament the fact that they never seem to have enough time. They suffer from a common problem—they can't say *no*. Why is it that one of the first words we learn to say as a child is the hardest word for many of us to say as an adult? When it comes to managing our time, *no* can be the greatest timesaving tool in the English language. We may be saying yes for the wrong reasons when . . .

☒ we want to gain the approval and acceptance of others.
☒ we are afraid of offending friends and acquaintances.
☒ we feel guilty for not measuring up to someone else's standards.
☒ being busy makes us feel important.
☒ we link overcommitment with spirituality.
☒ we agree because of low self-esteem.
☒ we have a compelling need to be needed by others.

Can a Woman Ever Say No? Yes, When . . .

☒ it leads to overcommitment, which in turn contributes to stress, burnout, and poor health.

☒ it distracts from our basic objectives.

☒ it results in the basic purposes of your calling not being fulfilled.

☒ it leaves you miserable. You find yourself saying, *why did I say I would do that?*

☒ it turns your joy to resentment.

☒ it means you don't have time to follow through (definitely unfair to the other person(s) involved!).

☒ it robs someone else of a blessing because you took on a project that God intended for someone else.

If You Do Say Yes

Unfortunately, people know "yessers" and take full advantage of them! The greater number of talents one possesses, the more essential is the ability to say no. In "Managing Your Life and Your Time," Jo Berry gives guidelines to follow before you say yes.

Breaking the habit of saying yes is a basic requirement for learning to say no. Saying yes is easier and more comfortable than saying no. We may be flattered or maybe we want to be liked. We say yes because we dislike confrontation, we don't want to hurt anyone, or we need acceptance.

Think before saying yes.

☒ *Evaluate* your motives and determine why you are saying yes.

☒ *Prioritize.* Pray, asking, *Is it God's will?*

- ☒ *Investigate.* Ask, what will it cost in terms of time, effort, and progress toward my goals?"
- ☒ *Consult* your calendar, asking how this fits with other plans and responsibilities.
- ☒ *Make sure* others are aware of your time demands. You can't expect friends to know your working hours or schedule if you don't communicate with them.
- ☒ *Respect* your own time as well as others' time. Don't let others establish your priorities. You will be held accountable to the Lord for how you spend your time.
- ☒ *Don't* be a "solve it all." Someone else's time problems are not your responsibility.

Actually Saying No

Here are some suggestions of how to say no the right way.

- ☒ *Don't offer excuses.* Do not launch into lengthy explanations. You're not asking for permission to decline; you are saying no.
- ☒ *Say no with tact and politeness.* Be considerate of other people's feelings. Thank the other person for asking you. Provide suggestions, new ideas, or other options if appropriate.
- ☒ *Develop a method of saying no.* Develop a specific *no* statement and practice saying it! *Say no clearly, kindly, and inoffensively.*
- ☒ *Stick with the decision you make.* Don't give in to the criticism that might result from saying no. Don't feel guilty about saying no. Remember, saying no may be God's will!

The biggest challenge facing Christian leaders is not separating the good from the bad, but taking the best out of all the good.

We need to learn that we must say no to some things that we really want to do in order to say yes to the very best things.

In a Nutshell
Test every situation or commitment you make before you agree to it by using these four questions:
1. Does God want me to do this?
2. Am I the right person?
3. Is this the right time?
4. Do I have enough information?

Realize that at times (for instance at work), you may not have an option to say no. We've all been given assignments that were a poor fit to our abilities, inherited responsibilities without full knowledge of all that was involved, or when nothing meshed time-wise. These circumstances simply have to be weathered. As leaders, however, we can work to avoid doing the same things to those under our supervision.

Why Don't We Delegate?
Moses is a good example of someone who was filling his time doing good things, yet not accomplishing the God-given tasks before him. It took his father-in-law, Jethro, to point out, "You cannot handle it alone" (Exodus 18:18). This incident sets the classic biblical precedent for delegation as a way of controlling one's time.

Jesus made use of this management skill. When sending out the disciples, He practiced the basic principles of training others. Mark 6 illustrates that Jesus taught and demonstrated what He wanted the disciples to do, sent them out to do it, and provided time for evaluation and encouragement.

ASK YOURSELF

Deep in your heart you probably know why you don't like to delegate. See if any of the following sounds like you:

- ☐ If I don't do it, no one will.
- ☐ No one else can do it as well as I can.
- ☐ If I delegate, I am giving up my authority or control.
- ☐ If someone else learns to do the task, I might not be needed anymore.
- ☐ Delegating means I can't do the job properly and need help.
- ☐ Asking others to do things will overwhelm them.
- ☐ Delegating takes too much time. It's quicker to do it myself.

Here are some tips to help you delegate more effectively:

- ☐ **Delegate** things you can't do efficiently.
- ☐ **Delegate** things that others can do better or with greater ease.
- ☐ **Delegate** things that are not a part of your primary goals or tasks.
- ☐ **Learn to ask for help.** Cut back on the quantity of your work.
- ☐ **Make sure** the individual understands exactly what you need done, but don't impose your methods.
- ☐ **Delegate** both responsibility and authority. Don't be guilty of running a one-woman show. When working with volunteers, give them responsibilities and authority to step out on their own. This will give them a sense of ownership.
- ☐ **Training** is a crucial part of delegation. Give the necessary information, remain available for questions, assist when needed, and offer praise and credit for a job well done.

☐ **Be considerate**. Take time to show someone how to do something, then follow up when necessary. When possible, assign tasks that relate to a person's interests and talents and rotate the less pleasant ones. Realize that delegating is time-consuming. It often takes more time to explain, instruct, and follow up than to do a task yourself, but there is a double payoff — both you and the delegate can benefit. Delegating builds teamwork.

Delegating and Leadership

If you fail to delegate, you'll end up worn out, and your results will be less than they should be. If you fail to delegate and train others, you cannot multiply yourself. You must set aside your personal reluctance to relinquish control and your perfection tendencies.

When I led a large team of women several years ago, I had to learn to let go of some things. I knew team members might not do things the way I would do them and might not have the same sense of urgency that I did. However, they were all committed to our purpose and were passionate about equipping women to grow spiritually and in ministry awareness. They learned and grew as leaders; the projects were finished; and women were encouraged. Many women's lives were touched by the ministry because I was willing to enlist others' help. All because of delegation! In *Organizing Your Day*, coauthor Sandra Felton said, "Good supervision is the art of getting average people to do superior work."

Leader Tip: For each project or activity, determine which tasks and responsibilities you can delegate.

LET'S TALK ABOUT INTERRUPTIONS

Leaders are often frustrated by interruptions. This could be because they have left too much to do in too little time. This can happen to a leader at church, in her workplace, with a community playhouse group, at a support group, or on a volunteer project for the homeless, and so on.

Did you know that it takes about 25 minutes to refocus after an interruption? No wonder you are dismayed by the co-worker who leans on your door and chats for ten minutes! It seems as if you'll never finish that presentation for work when your middle schooler interrupts you to go over his test questions. Or, maybe when your husband feels that because you are retired, your time is his.

I was talking to my second son recently on the phone and mentioned I was working on this book. I told him about the interruption statistic. He recalled a documentary he'd seen that talked about younger users of technology and how because things are geared to short spots of time, they enjoy jumping from one thing to another. He was of the opinion that because they are used to this, their recovery time is probably a lot shorter. So, if you are a younger leader, you will no doubt be more adept at moving back and forth with fewer difficulties!

There are two kinds of interruptions: *internal* and *external*. Internal interruptions are things like phone calls, meetings, visitors, fire drills, family emails, or social duties at work or home. External ones occur when you choose to read and answer emails or send Internet greeting cards when your focus should be elsewhere. I'm not saying these are unimportant activities, but when you are trying to write a presentation or organize next month's activities, they can be disruptive and annoying.

Workplace Interruptions

You may have a private office with a door that shuts, but you aren't allowed to close the door unless engaged in a confidential conversation. Your workspace may be a cubicle or a desk in an open office setting. Regardless of the setup of your space, here are several suggestions that might help you minimize interruptions.

✓ Isolate yourself as best you can.
✓ Block out time when you are the most productive and let others know you prefer not to be disturbed.
✓ Put your back to traffic if possible.
✓ If you have an assistant, give him or her specific guidelines about interruptions.
✓ Don't put a welcoming dish of candy on your desk!
✓ If someone asks for some of your time, schedule it for later, if possible.
✓ Silence your phone and ignore incoming emails when working on a project if allowed.
✓ If you are working at home, clarify with your family when you are available. Establish ground rules.
✓ Stand up when talking with someone and remain standing to discourage their staying too long.
✓ Remove chairs that encourage visitors to stay!

What About Me? I Work from Home

If you operate a business out of your home or work for someone else, you are in an especially vulnerable position. Some days you may feel like a sitting duck! It is important that you establish boundaries and guidelines for your family because interruptions are as disruptive at home as in the regular workplace.

More women are utilizing their time at home to their advantage. Commute time is eliminated, lunch money is saved, and babysitting fees are reduced. Hours spent on the computer or telephone can be very frustrating if family members and others don't respect your schedule. My oldest son spends one or two days per week working from home. His office is an alcove under the stairs. While small, it contains all he needs to work there. The family knows if Dad is in the alcove, he's working and is not to be disturbed.

You now have some techniques that can help you minimize interruptions. However, a word of caution is needed at this point: if your leadership position at work, church, or in the community requires a lot of networking and cooperative effort, you will need to be discerning about how or if you welcome interruptions. When they will help your team or group reach its goals, you need to use them in a positive way. Connecting and networking can't happen if you are never available!

Leader Tip: Finish this sentence: To avoid _____,
I will _____.

"Divine" Interruptions

There are times when interruptions should be treated as opportunities. Jesus never appeared to be without time for unscheduled interruptions. While on His way to see Jairus's

sick daughter, He was interrupted by another person in need
. . . not a ruler's child at the point of death, but an unclean,
chronically ill woman. He lovingly and patiently took the time
to heal the woman and to bless her, turning the interruption
into an opportunity.

Author Charles W. Shedd refers to "divine interruptions"
in *Time for All Things.* He concludes that one of the marks
of Christian greatness is a certain "interruptability." Certainly,
the parable of the Good Samaritan is a poignant reminder
of a Christian's responsibility to respond redemptively to
interruptions.

Look carefully at each interruption, asking God, "What
is it You want me to learn from this, or how do You want me
to respond to this, Father?" Try not to become irritated when
interruptions occur. The interrupter is more important than
the interruption, and God may want to you in that particular
situation and time. Of course, not every interruption is from
God, but almost all of them can be a learning experience if
our attitude is receptive rather than resentful. Offering them
to God can change them from irritations to victories!

LET'S TALK ABOUT PESKY PROCRASTINATION

As I held the small, round, wooden piece in my hands, I noticed
there were four letters embossed onto its surface: "TUIT." Oh,
I get it! Now I had gotten "around to it!"

Procrastination! Procrastination is defined as the art of
postponing things, putting them off until the last minute,
then rushing to finish them and sometimes not getting them
done at all. For some, it is the continued avoidance of starting
a task and seeing it to its conclusion. For others, it is a matter

of doing easier, low-priority chores instead of more difficult, high-priority tasks.

I sometimes wonder if even Paul himself didn't experience similar challenges. He wrote, "I have the desire to do what is good, but I cannot carry it out" (Romans 7:18). In our efforts to become more like the Master Manager we must gain control of our time by learning to deal with procrastination.

I have a wire "Out Box" on my desk. Actually, it's larger than a normal desk tray; it's an eight-inch deep basket (It holds *so* much more!). I use it as a temporary holder for items that need to be filed in the small cabinet under my desk, or in various binders and folders in my office or in the four-drawer filing cabinet that resides in our basement storage room. You already know where I'm going with this, don't you? Though items make it to the basement, they may not be filed. If I am in a hurry or feeling lazy, I put them on top of the cabinet!

Only last week I cleaned out the basket. I'd put off going down to the basement for weeks so my basket was overflowing. I filed some papers in the office cabinet, moved some folders around, but the pile for downstairs is still on top of my revolving bookcase! In the meantime, I'm not sure where my notes, speeches, and brochures are. Still in the basket? In the office stack? On top of the filing cabinet or actually filed away?

There is only one word that describes these actions: *procrastination!*

Any occasion is an occasion for procrastination—tax time, when the kitchen floor needs waxing, when it's time for routine medical exams. It is human nature to want to avoid things that are difficult, painful, or dull. For some people, procrastination is more than a bad habit. It is an almost paralyzing way of life.

We know that procrastination is rampant in our lives, so why do we do it? What can we learn about procrastination that will help us avoid it? Fear is the "bottom line" of a lot of our procrastinations. As you read, decide if any of these describe you.

1. **Fear of failure.** Many procrastinators fear being judged by others or are too hard on themselves. They are afraid they will be found lacking and that even their best efforts won't be good enough.

   These people feel their worth depends solely on how well they perform. They do not want to try anything until they know exactly how everything will work. Ironically, when the procrastinator finally moves, there is no hope of doing an outstanding job. By her delay the procrastinator tries to avoid disappointing herself by falling short of her goals.

2. **Fear of success.** Other procrastinators worry about what will happen if they do manage to do a first-class job. Their fears are rooted in the mistaken notion that success can only bring trouble. Some fear that success might put them in the spotlight where they will be vulnerable to criticism or abuse. Others fear that success might leave them no time to relax. These delayers conclude that, by waiting, they can get the project done in less time and the unused time can be spent on relaxation.

3. **Fear of being controlled.** Many people procrastinate because they want to feel they are in control. It is a way of saying, "You can't make me do this." In this situation a procrastinator's self-worth is based on her not conforming.

4. **Fear of separation.** For some, procrastination is a way of maintaining closeness with others. They put things off, do poorly, and ask for endless advice as a way of keeping others attached to them. Some delay in order to maintain a dependent relationship with someone. For example, a divorced woman may procrastinate on all her financial matters because doing it herself means admitting that she is really on her own.

5. **Fear of attachment.** Procrastination can serve as a means of keeping people at a safe distance, protecting one from intimate relationships. No one wants to get involved with someone whose life seems to always be on the brink of disaster, someone with outstanding debts, a rundown car, a messy house.

6. **Other fears.** These could be fears of confrontation, the unknown, and facing reality. The Book of Acts gives an account of Governor Felix's procrastination as the result a fearful reaction to Paul: 'That's enough for now! You may leave. When I find it convenient, I will send for you'" (Acts 24:25).

> *"Today is the tomorrow we worried about yesterday."*
>
> — UNKNOWN
>
> *"You can't change what you don't acknowledge."*
>
> — DR. PHIL MCGRAW

Change Your Behavior!

There are several ways to modify your behavior once you've decided to stop procrastinating. Use the following exercises to help you minimize the round TUIT lifestyle.

☒ Since we all do it, analyze your procrastination history. Write down two or three examples of times you've procrastinated recently. Describe the circumstances and try to identify the motive. Record the excuses you made. Try to get a clear picture of your particular brand of procrastination.

☒ Make a list of all the tasks you tend to put off repeatedly. Prioritize that list from the most to the least important. Can some of these tasks be delegated? Can some be dropped or can you trade a task to another person?

☒ Set reasonable, specific, concrete, and reachable goals. Break big jobs into manageable chunks, then do them one by one. Describe how you can do this on one of your current projects.

☒ Visualize the benefits of completing your project. Promise yourself a reward and follow through when your goal has been achieved. Don't wait for praise from others (it may never come!), but reward yourself for a job well done. List a reward you're going to give yourself for a task completed.

☒ Enlist the support of others as you battle procrastination. Tell someone what you are working on and when you want to complete it. If you know someone with a goal similar to yours, make a plan together. Call each other for support when you are tempted to quit or need help getting unstuck.

☒ Learn to relax. Learn to be calm when you feel yourself tensing, rushing, panicking. Use scheduled time for leisure and recreation to energize you to action. Write (yes, right now!) some relaxation time into your schedule.

☒ Recognize that energy levels vary throughout the day. If you are a morning person, schedule work on tough, important jobs during your prime time. Schedule easier tasks when you are less attentive. Make a list for tomorrow and schedule according to your energy level.

☒ "Unschedule" some of your already-committed activities. Procrastinators often plan too much, overestimating the time they have available, and underestimating the time it takes to do a job. Make a schedule of daily activities and put in all the things you are already committed to doing or what you think you might be doing. What changes need to take place to provide more time in your schedule?

☒ Use even little bits of time wisely. Name a project you've never started because you've said you haven't had the full amount of time it will take to complete the project. Now divide it into smaller time blocks.

Questions to Ask Yourself About Your Procrastination Habits

OK, now you have some possible reasons for your procrastination. You've read what steps you can take to limit procrastinating. With this knowledge ask yourself some questions — and answer honestly! These questions might make you focus on some specific areas that give you trouble.

- Do you put things away quickly?
- Do you find yourself facing a lot of emergencies because you didn't take action earlier?
- What price have you paid for procrastinating?
- Do you think most of your tasks are too large and overwhelming?
- Do you get too involved emotionally in your tasks?
- Do you ever think about what you could or should delegate?

If you leave these questions to answer later, you might be procrastinating!

WHAT ABOUT YOU?

List four things in your daily life that you habitually put off. Why?

Name three goals you've set but are delaying action on. Why?

Choose a time to work on each of these areas. Write down a target time and post it where you will see it frequently.

Leader Tip: Organize all your workspaces so that your procrastination habits begin to decrease.

ENTER THE ELEPHANT

While a day still has 24 hours and a week has 7 days, how we use that time, what we expect of ourselves and others has dramatically been revolutionized. You probably know that I am thinking about that elephant called technology again. And, you are right!

As in other discussions about technology, the question always arises about whether it is a blessing or an intrusion in our lives. The answer is a two-sided coin. Mobile phones connect us more and more with others in a variety of ways. If we don't have time to actually make a call, we can text brief messages, reply almost instantly, and do it more frequently than any of us ever dreamed.

Now is a good time to analyze our use of technology as it relates to time management. In the previous chapter we talked about how our expectations have soared because of what can be accomplished with technology. But these expectations put a new burden on us. We realize our need to communicate quickly, frequently, and to train and supervise others even at a distance. My son, who works for a structural engineering company, has a supervisor who works from his home in another part of the state. They plan by way of emails, submit project work by way of computer, and work together to design in 3-D because of rapidly-developing software, rarely talking face-to-face.

When we assume leadership responsibilities we will be challenged to do more in shorter periods of time. Technology can be our friend obviously, but we must be careful about managing our time as we use it. It is easy to try to pull things off with no time to spare. Leaders are not exempt from this malady. We try to switch from project to project, and while we may be exhilarated by the adrenaline, our work may suffer.

It won't take our followers or employees long to figure out that we are trying to take shortcuts to get desired results. Regardless of the "look" of a presentation with technological bells and whistles, people working with us want to see sound research, thoughtful insights, and be motivated to participate or agree with our proposal.

Leaders need to be examples to others. With regard to delegation, interruptions, procrastination, and multitasking leaders are expected to be more adept. Switching gears constantly is not a good model for co-workers. Procrastination has been the undoing of many leaders, resulting in missed deadlines, which affect everyone, and creating unnecessary tension. Multitasking is something every leader should learn. Leaders need to know how to logically put activities together for maximum results.

Whether you are leading a group of women at church, developing a team to sponsor a breast cancer awareness fair, or working with women wanting to firm and tone their muscles at a YWCA, you can use wait time, and take the small amounts of time that come your way to increase your effectiveness. Modeling this behavior helps others develop their time management skills.

Leading by example, there are several simple things leaders can do to teach others to manage their time:

- Don't leave out unfinished projects. A cluttered desk tells others there's a lot going on and it hasn't been done!
- Use your mobile device to remind you of appointments, calendar dates, and so on.
- Use short breaks to do mindless tasks as a way of relaxing when working on a big project. You might go through accumulated junk mail as a way of resting your eyes and brain.

Leader Tip: Don't be so concerned with all the balls in your air that you neglect those you are trying to lead.

TECHNOLOGY, TIME, AND MY LEADERSHIP ABILITIES

Use the following exercise to evaluate how technology impacts your use of time.

- Think about your cell phone usage: does it help you manage your time more effectively? Name three things you do on your phone on a regular basis.
- How do you view incoming emails, text messages, and faxes? As interruptions or as a means of being a better leader?
- How does advanced technology help you be a more effective leader? List specific examples.

Henry David Thoreau said, "I say, let your affairs be as two or three, and not a hundred or a thousand; instead of a million count half a dozen, and keep your accounts on your thumbnail."

Thoreau obviously didn't have as much to do as we women do today! We are constantly looking for new ways to save time. Now, we all know you can't save time, but we try anyway. Are you addicted to the adrenaline rush that comes from a pressing deadline? I worked with an individual who, even though deadlines were set for everyone, his personal deadlines were nebulous. The bigger the project, the later he seemed to be in getting his assignments done. While everyone else was chewing their nails, this person blithely sailed along until the looming deadline's wave bore down on our collective boat threatening to sink it. He may have gotten a rush out of the process, but his co-workers certainly didn't!

You may feel as if you have no idle time in an average day, when in actuality, you probably do. It's similar to that study about leisure time mentioned earlier in this chapter. Since we can't save time, perhaps we should consider some ways we can redeem time. Redeeming time is not difficult, but it takes planning like everything else.

When we visited our sons last fall, I watched our busy daughter-in-law as she packed for the day. With three children in three different schools, she was on the road every day. She carried her master calendar and smartphone so she could look things up on the spot. She had a knitting bag with a current project and knitted as she watched soccer games. She carried bills to pay as she waited in the doctor's office. While waiting at Irish dance practice, she handled the finances related to the group's performances.

What was she doing? She was redeeming her time. She was making use of "idle time" during her day. There was nothing frenzied about her movements; she was purposeful; she was where she had to be but was not fretting about what was left undone at home.

Rather than standing still while you wait somewhere, try some of these ideas to redeem your idle time.

- **Take something to do wherever you go.** Knit an afghan, hem a skirt, cut out bulletin board letters, write thank-you notes, catch up on emails and texts, or plan your weekly menus.
- **Use regular idle time to your advantage.** As you commute, listen on audio to the Book of Proverbs, pray for your family and friends, think through a problem, or call your mother (only if you have hands-free cell phone capability!).
- **Eliminate idle time if you can.** Call ahead to confirm appointments and if things are on time. Do all your errands

at one time, routing them in order so you don't have to backtrack.

☒ **Consolidate time when possible.** Put similar things together as you plan your day. For example, if you have three things relating to a community project to do, combine them into one action.

☒ **Don't offend others by "always doing something."** My father once asked, "Don't you ever sit still and do nothing?" I shook my head sheepishly as I continued to crochet a baby blanket. I was there to visit, and he wanted my attention. Redeeming your time while at a committee meeting is inappropriate, as is giving someone only half your attention at lunch as you answer accumulated text messages.

☒ **Keep a list** of short, easy-to-do projects and do them as you wait on hold for the insurance agent, such as emptying the dishwasher, cleaning out a desk drawer, and so on.

IS WHAT I DO "SWITCH-TASKING" OR BENIGN MULTITASKING?

Peter Bregman in his book, *18 Minute Manager*, asserts that people who are distracted by incoming emails, texts, and phone messages test 10 IQ points less than those who are not. Research indicates that this is the same decrease as a person who loses a night's sleep. Productivity takes a dive as much as 40 percent. Heavy multitaskers are less competent than others who only multitask occasionally.

Bregman claims that most multitaskers are really "switch-taskers," which is inefficient and unproductive. I start out believing I'll get a lot done when in actuality the results of switch tasking fall below what I wanted them to be.

Benign multitasking is the mindless activities that we link to something enjoyable. Watching her daughter play soccer is something my daughter-in-law enjoys, but rather than sit with her hands idle, she chooses to knit an afghan for a college-bound niece. I enjoy listening to all kinds of music so I used to turn the volume high and clean house as I hummed along. When "Dueling Banjos" was first released, I cleaned in record time!

WHAT ABOUT YOU?

Write down one task you have on a regular basis. Answer the following questions to determine if you can simplify your system or be more organized.

Is there a faster way to do this?

Does this task need doing at all?

Could someone else do it as well or better?

Can it be postponed until a better time?

Do you have a specific place for most things?

Are you logical about your storage or do you "clear the decks?"

FINAL THOUGHTS ABOUT MANAGING YOUR TIME

Often, with the demands of everyday life, we lose sight of our goals and get sidetracked by things that don't really matter. The urgent demands seem to cry out for our immediate response, and the most important tasks go unattended. When this happens, God's will becomes fuzzy, like a photograph taken with an improperly focused camera.

You are familiar with the story of Mary and Martha, Lazarus's sisters. Let's look again at the scriptural account of one of Jesus' visits to their home, which serves as an illustration for this final discussion on time management.

⚜ WE NEED ⚜

Identify priorities. The story of Mary and Martha provides an excellent example of how easy it is to have a faulty focus on priorities. Martha must have had the gift of hospitality. She was the one responsible for entertaining the guests, for making them feel welcomed. She must have felt that it was a real privilege that the

Lord would choose her home to rest and recuperate. Making her guests comfortable was a priority for her.

Her sister, Mary, sat at the Lord's feet listening to what He said while Martha was hustling about. She probably was so attuned to His words that she wasn't even aware of what was going on around her. Martha, on the other hand, became so wrapped up in what she was doing that her activities distracted her from the Lord. Her focus was faulty; her priorities were out of line.

Like many of you, I let life distract me from the Lord. All of us, at one time or another, have become so involved in what we are doing that we forget for whom we are doing it.

The more Martha thought about the situation, the angrier she got and the more self-righteous she felt. Finally, Martha could keep silent no longer. She had to say something! Martha vented her frustration by condemning others who were not as active. She accused Jesus of not caring and before He had a chance to respond, she told Him what to do! She thought she knew better than the Lord or Mary what her sister's priorities should be.

Aren't we a little like Martha? How often do we tell God what is best for us? We criticize what others do when actually our own priorities are the ones out of focus.

Limit priorities. Most of us have so many priorities that we are weighted down by the volume of the many important and demanding things in our lives. From God's perspective, only a few things in life deserve our intense attention or concern. What a relief! Jesus cautions against overloading our minds and schedules with an excess of unnecessary things. He reminded Martha that everything in life is not of equal significance.

Some things are more important than others. As was true for Martha, most of the things we get worked up over aren't that important in the overall scheme of life.

Choose the best. When we place ourselves at Jesus' feet and relinquish our time to Him, He shows us what is necessary and what isn't, and what our personal priorities should be. Knowing our priorities and acting upon them are two different things, however. Notice Jesus' words to Martha: "Mary has chosen what is better" (Luke 10:42). Mary made a choice about how she would spend her time, a choice to focus on her priority. Many of us are like Martha and choose to get sidetracked by the cries of the urgent tasks around us.

Managing our time in a Christlike fashion involves making a series of choices, choices about what is important, when to slow down, when to ask for help, when to say yes, and when to say no. You can choose to gain control of your time, like the Master Manager, as you seek to choose the good things. The choice is yours!

4 GROUP-BUILDING ESSENTIALS

By Judy Hamlin

The existence of groups means several things for women's lives. We may enjoy the groups of which we are a part, or we might find ourselves reluctantly attending a group function that means little to us. Why the difference? Your answer will vary depending on the group, its leaders, or its members. The response you give may have nothing to do with any of this but with yourself and your personal situation.

If you are a member of a group and are hesitant to stay with the group, that's one thing. However, if you are the leader of the group, you are in trouble! I guess congratulations are in order if you're the leader!

DEFINING GROUP

Definitions

> "A group is a collection of individuals whose existence
> as a collection is rewarding to the individuals."
> —BERNARD BASS IN TEAM LEADERSHIP, BY K. O. GANGEL

> "A Christian group can be defined as a gathering of believers with natural interests working towards a common goal."
>
> —*Feeding and Leading: A Practical Handbook on Administration in Churches and Christian Organizations*, by K. O. GANGEL

> A group: "a number of people who work together or share certain beliefs."
>
> —*Miriam Webster's Dictionary*

There are many different kinds of groups. Special interest groups, support groups, age- or interest-based groups, and work-related groups are examples. Many other words are substitutes for the word "group" such as *class, category, lot, batch, kind,* or *variety.* In a commercial setting the group might be a team, an association, a club or society, a guild, circle, or union. There are musical groups: bands and ensembles. My brother, a professional violinist, is a member of Moonsville Collective, a group committed to revitalizing American folk music.

You may have joined a crew to make a parade float, or a league of some sort. Perhaps an army of volunteers wanting to help the homeless. Groups of people include enclaves, lobbies, mobs, bunches, packs, sets, cliques, and communities. Even gaggles (no, evidently it can be people, too, not only geese)!

Did you find yourself in any of these groups or in one I missed? Most likely. Have you led any of these groups? Maybe. Regardless of the type or purpose of a group, there are some overriding leadership principles all leaders must know, as well as skill sets a leader must use to ensure that the group is productive. This means that the group becomes a meaningful collection of persons united by a common goal.

Leadership means more than showing up to host a meeting, being a project leader, or coordinating an event. It calls for women who will exercise both acquired and God-given skills, and who will develop practical understanding so they can effectively lead those who follow them. Understanding the dynamics of group interaction will help you build a group that functions as it should.

In this chapter, small groups are defined as people with similar interests or needs. Groups exist for a number of reasons and serve a variety of purposes while functioning according to their reasons for existence.

WHY DO GROUPS EXIST?

Don't we have enough to do without another "something" that takes up our time? Surely, we can eliminate all that stuff relating to groups — things such as membership, goals, objectives, training, and oh yes, the meetings. I've attended too many group meetings to count, and I can tell you they weren't all they were advertised to be! Unfortunately, most of them were unproductive and completely without any redeeming features.

Why then, do we continue to form groups, join groups, and admonish others to participate? The essence of a healthy functioning group is that it should be an encouraging factor in our lives. Groups have value in women's eyes because they are the place where lifelong friendships are established and women find support for the life issues that challenge them. For many women it is the only place where they receive affirmation of their worth. Groups help solve problems, provide networks and hours of enjoyment. A woman is motivated to make changes, improve her skills, and develop as a leader in her home, community, workplace, and church.

All of these things can (and should) happen within a group. What marvelous benefits! And, that's in addition to the actual purpose of the group. The opportunity to make a difference, to contribute to a cause, or to influence others sometimes takes a back seat to the confidence women can develop as a result of associating with other women whose experiences, backgrounds, and beliefs model lifestyles that appeal to them.

Experiences in any group can build meaningful relationships as well as providing accountability opportunities. Part of your job as a leader is to help members apply what they have learned within the group and challenge them to grow and mature. You may lead a group of community volunteers or a task force at work. An effective group needs not only to achieve its purpose and reach its goals, but its members' lives should be enriched. The beginning and end of groups has to be more than the assignment.

The additional dimension Christian women's groups have helps to transform women's lives as they move beyond themselves and develop a worldview that sees the world as needy and lost, waiting to learn about God's love. As women grow spiritually and reach new levels of competence and compassion, the impact they have on their world is immeasureable.

Well, having said all of this, the rest of this chapter will focus on why women join groups, what being a group member means, how groups work, the mechanics of group dynamics, being an effective group leader, and how to evaluate your groups. That's quite an assignment for one chapter! If you have the time, read the remainder of the chapter in sections, and complete each evaluation as you go to maximize the value of the information in each section.

WHY WOMEN JOIN GROUPS

Emily Morrison, in her book *Leadership Skills*, discusses reasons why people—in our case, women—join groups. Something must draw women to participate in this "collection" of individuals. Why? Here are some reasons.

It's OK for her to be there. She doesn't necessarily have to bring influence, power, or money with her. Illustration: Margaret didn't learn to read until she was an adult. You couldn't ask her to read a verse of Scripture without notice. She had no developed skills; she had no understanding of world issues. She had no money to support mission causes. But Margaret did have a willing heart to continue to learn as best she could. She was a prayer warrior, asking when my conferences were so she could be on her knees praying for me. Margaret joined our group because it was OK for her to be there.

She believes in the cause. She can see that the group's purpose aligns with the purposes she has in her own life. That could mean being an advocate for children, equipping other women in life skills, or working in a pregnancy crisis center.

She can have input. Her opinions count; others listen to her. She has a part in the direction of the group.

Her needs are met and the group's activities are of interest to her. She won't join a group where she finds no one her age, nor one that is totally passive in its makeup. If it's a caring group, she'll find encouragement and love. If it's a learning group, she will apply new concepts in her life. If it's a serving group, she'll be involved in those outreach activities.

WHY WOMEN LEAVE GROUPS

Because women are extremely busy, they may go in and out of groups for a variety of reasons. The following list is especially true for women who volunteer by the thousands to work with children, youth, the handicapped, women trying to break the cycle of poverty, and in a myriad of other ministries, both religious and civic.

☒ They can't see that their participation is making a difference.

☒ The group's purpose has changed.

☒ The group isn't (seemingly) concerned about meeting their needs.

☒ They are not given any opportunity to contribute their creativity or participate in decision-making.

☒ There are no opportunities for personal growth.

WHY DOES SHE ACT THAT WAY?

Regardless of the type of group you lead or join, you've met the woman whose presence frustrates you and makes you wonder how you'll be able to lead past, over, or around her. Because women join groups for a wide variety of reasons as we've already discussed, it's easy to see that while on the surface everyone might seem the same, it simply isn't true.

My reason for joining the church's babysitting co-op was simple: I needed a break from my children! My thought process when I joined a young women's mission organization was a bit more complicated: I felt compelled by God to participate and enjoyed every moment as we reached out to people needing God's love. When I joined a community war-relief project group in my small town, I was motivated by a love for the soldiers and my country.

As I think back over my participation in different groups, I can see in my mind the other women who were present. We weren't all the same age; we didn't all attend the same church; some were shy while others, like me, were talkers. I'm not sure I know what motivated each of them to join the groups, but we were united by a common purpose most of the time.

On the other hand, I once led a group where several members came with personal agendas that didn't always match our assignment and purpose. It was a difficult challenge as I tried to assess members' motivation, behavior, and attitude. Because this group related to a large denominational structure, I knew it was important to identify the members' spiritual gifts so we could build a strong group together.

Please understand that discovery of spiritual gifts does not always lead to understanding or effective use of those gifts. People need to know how a spiritual gift relates to their lives, to others, to their church, and to the Lord's will for them. Study the New Testament to find descriptions of spiritual gifts, then think about your group members. Books such as Barbara Joiner's *Yours for the Giving*, can help you understand gifts from the biblical perspective, and see ways God uses gifted people in His church today.

HOW TO BE BETTER GROUP MEMBERS

It isn't the group leader alone who has responsibilities. Members have roles to fill also. Morrison discusses the various ways group members can be better participants. These can be applied to any type of group—community task forces, church study groups, ministry projects, neighborhood groups, or teams at work.

⊠ Come to the meeting prepared.

⊠ Arrive on time.

⊠ Stay until the end of the meeting.

⊠ Be attentive, not making lists for the next day or reading a magazine.

⊠ Be perceptive and alert to what is happening.

⊠ Help facilitate discussions. Don't simply sit there!

⊠ Be a contributor, either with comments or an interested look on your face. Even nodding your head is good!

⊠ Don't be afraid to disagree. If you don't comment in the meeting, don't take that liberty later.

⊠ Don't be afraid to be creative.

⊠ Give other ideas a fair chance. They might be better than yours!

⊠ Become more tentative—i.e., less certain or dogmatic in your views.

Here are some additional guidelines to remember when trying to be a good group member:

1. Speak only for yourself.
2. Respect others. Listen (i.e. don't have side conversations).
3. Limit your sharing. Others may want to have input too.
4. Take responsibility and complete your assignments.
5. Help the group stay on the subject.
6. Be faithful in your attendance. Notify the leader if you can't be present.
7. Remember the importance of confidentiality.

EVALUATE YOUR GROUP

- **Make a list** of the members of a group you lead or in which you participate. What unique contribution does each person make to the group because of their personality?
- **Identify** the spiritual gifts of three group members.
- If you are the group leader, how can you **encourage** members to use their gifts?

WHAT MAKES GROUP MEMBERS TICK?

The answer is *group mechanics* — communication, group involvement, and consensus on the group's direction. These elements involve action, participation, and cooperation among all the group's members. The more that good group mechanics are employed, the greater the increase in understanding, retention, involvement, and enjoyment of group members.

Now that we've taken a brief look at groups and their value, we need an understanding of the group member. Enlisting women to participate in something larger than what they can do alone is the mark of an effective leader. Understanding the differences you'll find in individual members will help you be more strategic in what you try to accomplish and how you work with them.

Look at the following group mechanics to help you understand your role as group leader, improve your leadership skills, and discover ways to use these components to make your group a success.

Communication. One of the most important processes that takes place in a group is communication.

☒ In a healthy group, members actively listen to one another.

☒ To be a good communicator, you must be a good listener.

☒ Learning to listen is the most basic skill of communication. A good listener:

✓ allows others to complete their sentences without interrupting

✓ does not silently contradict the speaker

✓ gives the speaker full attention, hearing what the speaker says the first time

✓ is aware of other communication modes besides verbal ones

✓ does not give an opinion before it is asked for

✓ looks at the person who is speaking

☒ When you are speaking, remember how easily others can miss your point.

☒ The listener's interpretation of what you say travels through experience and preconceived ideas.

☒ Make sure you keep your comments simple, repeating if necessary.

As the leader of the group, you have the responsibility to use good communication. You can, by your example, encourage healthy communication among group members and make it a group characteristic.

An important element in communication within a group is the effective use of technology. Carefully crafted email messages or brief text messages as meeting reminders can be used effectively if you are intentional in what you say, how you say it, and how clear your meaning is. Recognize that there will probably be some misunderstandings along the way!

Diversity in group involvement. Because we are not all alike, diversity in any group will have an impact on its make-up and its accomplishments. Any leader who disregards diversity will be making a costly mistake. A casual glance at any women's group reveals differences. Cultural differences may be apparent. There may be a variety in ages among its members. If you listen closely, you might hear varying speech. Observe a meeting in progress and you might even detect differing thought patterns and approaches to problem-solving.

What we see above the surface are language, physical features, clothing, and customs, even food preferences. Most of who women are is not on the surface, however. Like an iceberg, there is much more under the surface. What we don't see are attitudes, beliefs and values, perceptions, learning styles, and thought patterns. While diversity is a wonderful, enriching aspect of leading and building groups, there are many challenges that come with it.

The very things that can enrich a group's effectiveness can stymy its use of resources. As a leader you need to encourage members to listen to each other and regard others' input. Don't allow an "in-out" group mentality to develop. By this I mean, it is unhealthy if there is an attitude that "*They* pushed the idea through. The rest of *us* didn't have anything to say about it." This can happen very easily in women's groups because all of us have a tendency to be closer to women with similar life situations or interests. The division may be age-related: older women in one sub-group, younger women in another. Working women may feel isolated or single women might feel left out.

What can you as a leader do to both foster and manage your group's diversity?

☒ Create awareness of the group's diversity. Acknowledge what diversity can bring to the group.

☒ Improve your group's skills in processing the issues that arise from diversity. For example, communication is one area where misunderstanding can easily occur when differing cultural values are present.

☒ Work to create a safe environment for all group members. Your group will grow only if members feel it is a safe place to share their opinions, beliefs, and ideas.

One of the most rewarding experiences I've ever had was working to establish a culturally diverse group of women that would promote personal involvement in missions-related ministries. Developing language subgroups was both challenging and rewarding. Learning about various cultures and hearing their ideas enriched our group beyond anything we'd expected. We learned to respect each other, turn to each other for help, and to support the women with whom they worked within their language group. Our passion was the same, but it played out differently in each culture. What a group it was!

Whether you lead a group at work or a special project for your teen's high school booster club, you will do well to look toward building a group that is intentionally diverse. By this I mean, there should be diversity in age, cultural background, experience, and perhaps even gender. Diversity can help you accomplish group purposes and goals because each member brings something unique to the group. You will need to lead members to establish emotional bonds, communicate clearly with others, and share their experiences.

The value of this came home to me and a short-term missions team when we traveled to Croatia to participate in a national women's event and to teach leadership skills. We came together from two states, and our team had a Latino pastor's wife, a senior citizen, a young stay-at-home mother of preschoolers, a denominational leader, and another single woman. Little did we know that the Croatian leadership team wanted such a team! Even though they hadn't put their request in writing, God knew what was needed to meet the Croatian women's needs. We were more effective because of the desired diversity.

Direction of the group. We have already said that groups need to have a purpose for existing, and group members need to know what that purpose is. If your group is through your church or faith-based, its leader needs to identify biblical principles and practices that apply to your group. Members might help to write guidelines for areas such as prayer, openness, affirmation, availability of group members to one another, and requirements and accountability of group members.

Answering these questions might help you to determine the direction of your group:

- ☒ How was your group formed? If it was formed to meet a specific need, such as improvement of reading skills among elementary students, reassigning office duties, or promoting involvement in a missions project, a leader should clarify the purpose so members know how relate to each other and to the group.
- ☒ What is the common purpose of the group?
- ☒ What goals do group members share? Common goals are essentials elements in a group.

☒ What external factors influence the group? (Attendance may vary according to the time of the year if there are seasonal projects, and so on.)

☒ Would a group or team covenant benefit your group? Poll group members and list reasons for and against the covenant concept, and vote on the matter. If a covenant is used, avoid making it too long, binding, or restrictive.

What do you think about this statement?

> "If you don't know where you're going, any path will get you there, but you won't realize if you're lost, You won't know what time you'll arrive, You won't know the dimensions of your challenge, others won't understand how they could help, and since you could pass right by without recognizing it, you won't get the satisfaction of having arrived!"
>
> —JIM LUNDY, *T.E.A.M.S.*

EVALUATE YOUR GROUP

Which of these arrows best represents the direction of one of your groups? Which arrow would you choose to represent the group a year from now?

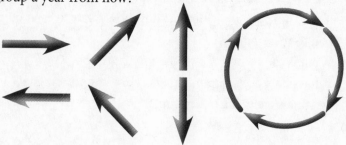

As you begin to focus on groups and their structure, there are several other areas you might consider:

GROUP DIVERSITY

We've already discussed the diversity you will find in the makeup of groups. Aside from the differences members bring to a group setting, the group as a whole will be diverse too. Diversity can produce sound consensus decisions, but remember that a diverse group is more difficult to lead. Be prepared to work at developing this leadership skill!

Group-makeup diversity: Your group could possibly have members whose first language is other than English. Generational differences and background experiences will add to the complexity of your group.

Task diversity: If you are selecting people to work on a task group, choose both task- and relationship-oriented members. The task people will guarantee the job gets done; the relationship people will make sure decisions reflect sensitivity and compassion.

Group-size diversity: Task groups should be small, no fewer than five, no more than seven members. Even numbers are undesirable, as that could result in divided votes. More than seven members makes it difficult for everyone to contribute.

GROUP GROWTH

Groups naturally go through stages of development. While these stages vary from group to group, some form of developmental process often takes place. Students of group psychology describe these stages with various titles. Using Kevin

Thompson's explanations from his manual for small-group ministry, these stages might be described as:

- *The first stage* when members look to the leader for help and direction. The leader is uncertain about how much freedom to give members.
- *A second stage* when the leader begins to prepare members to accept more responsibility, and members tend to resist or be anxious about this responsibility.
- *The third stage* when members try to gain independence and recognition. They often reject the leader, and ignore or contradict the leader's suggestions. At this stage the leader needs maturity to accept these attitudes and avoid a power struggle.
- *A fourth stage* when members gain confidence in themselves, and celebrate by enjoying the group and ignoring the leader. The wise leader will recognize this stage and allow the group to develop and grow.
- *A final, productive stage* when members accept the leader and are ready to move forward as a productive team. In this stage shared leadership begins to take shape, and often the leader is able to allow the group to move forward on its own.

GROUP MEETINGS

You may be a new leader assuming a position on a task force at work, or leading a group of women making quilts for a hospice, or coordinating a ministry at your church. If you have experience in leadership, a new role won't create a problem for you. However, if you've never begun a new group or led one before, it can be a daunting task. Look at the following list of components for effective meetings. If you don't accomplish anything in a meeting, something is obviously wrong. Meetings are not for people who have nothing better to do with their time!

☒ **Start on time.**

☒ **Begin with prayer.**

☒ **Have a written agenda**, give members a copy, and follow it. You, the leader, should guide the meeting time. For business and planning sessions, restrict attendance to the core decision-making group. Visitors should be excluded at a meeting where you are leading strategy discussions.

(The agenda should include all pertinent upcoming dates, restate the purpose if necessary, allocated time for discussions, and action plan to implement group decisions.)

☒ **Pay attention** to the different thought processes within your group, allowing extra time in case clarification is needed. Keep the group focused on one topic at a time to minimize confusion and jumping ahead. In other words, no rabbit-chasing allowed!

☒ **Make sure the meeting environment** is comfortable and conducive for the business you need to transact.

☒ **Try to involve everyone.** Don't allow a few to dominate discussions.

☒ **Keep your expectations reasonable.** Decide what is ideal and what is reality.

☒ **Make assignments, establish deadlines,** and make sure decisions are clear to everyone.

☒ **End on time.**

I THINK I SEE THAT ELEPHANT

Every leader struggles to facilitate meetings, whether they are large or small, and to make meetings productive. Using technology at any meeting can be a challenge. Why? Leaders need to make the technology relevant and pertinent to the topics being addressed at the meeting and not overwhelm those present with information.

While technology advances and changes, its use can bring new and fresh dimensions to our meetings. The hazard of too much technology or poor usage of it can be a hindrance, however. For example, if all the bells and whistles of a visual presentation overwhelm the information, technology is a hindrance rather than a supportive meeting element.

Many meetings are held for instructional purposes (new procedures, new products, restructuring, organizational issues, and so on). Here are some ways to make these meetings productive and memorable (taken from *Corporate and Incentive Travel*, August 2010).

- **Know** your audience and tailor your technological use to match it — Generational differences will determine how effective your technology is. Try to accommodate everyone.
- **Pay attention** to your environment — Seating arrangements, noise, and even lighting help or can be detrimental to learning.
- **Nutritionists** tell us that starchy foods can produce fatigue and "brain fog." A lot of sugar could give your meeting an unexpected "high!"
- **Match** your meeting objectives with technology. If you are providing basic information, technology can be effective.

If your focus is on making decisions or learning advanced skills, these may be best received in person.

- **Don't plan long sessions.** The use of time is critical in having successful, productive meetings. Use your time wisely.
- **Vary** your delivery formats during the meeting. Consider everyone's learning-style preferences.
- **Realize** that group participation can increase productivity. Provide opportunities for input and discussion during your meeting.
- **Presentations** should require the group to use more than the hearing sense.
- **Create** special times for social interaction because most of us want to know what others think and feel.
- **Stay informed** about new technology. Attendees like to see that their leaders are staying abreast of new ways of imparting information.

SETTING THE STAGE FOR SUCCESSFUL GROUP MEETINGS

It may seem like a small thing, but if you pay attention to the meeting environment, your rate of successful meetings will increase. Creating a welcoming environment is a key element in building a healthy group. **Room arrangement** affects interaction and participants' comfort. Where meeting program participants or **speakers stand** determines whether the meeting is formal or informal. For women, **room temperature** is an element not to be disregarded. Too hot? Not good. Too cold? Not good either. Attention wonders when attendees are not comfortable! **Preparation** is crucial. Women can always find something else to do so they won't put up with lack of preparation on your part as the leader or others' roles as speaker, project manager, or even the refreshment coordinator.

Planned breaks will help participants refocus after a period of time sitting. As leader, it is your job to schedule breaks. **Food** served should match the occasion for the meeting. If you are having a keynote speaker and women are coming directly from work, provide something more substantial. If the meeting's purpose is to work on a community project and requires supplies, tables, and up-and-down activity, finger food will be appropriate. If your meeting is scheduled to last more than two hours, healthy food is necessary to sustain energy levels. Minimize sugar intake for a calmer meeting!

One last detail that will move your meetings toward being more effective is the use of **name tags**. The growth of your group will be related to how friendly and welcoming the current members and you the leader are. Remembering others' names is important and lets them know you care they are present. Everyone likes to be called by name, and name tags help newcomers feel welcome.

EVALUATE HOW YOU ARE DOING

Use the checklist below to evaluate your first group meeting.
10–12 checks = successful meeting
7–9 checks = work on areas needing attention for the future
Fewer than 7 checks = rethink your agenda and proceedings
_____ Started on time
_____ Ended on time
_____ Atmosphere was nonthreatening
_____ Discussion allowed everyone to participate

_____ Group purpose and goals were agreed upon

_____ All points of view were encouraged

_____ Questions of judgment were decided by the group

_____ Agenda items were brief and clear

_____ Proceedings were orderly

_____ Unclear statements were clarified

_____ Creative thinking resulted

_____ Decisions were made and a plan formulated

GROUP-BUILDING IDEAS

Members need to work with you to develop a group bond. The following resources may help you create that bond.

☒ Ideas or women's groups: juliabettencourt.com (Creative Ladies Ministries)

☒ Use "Chase's Calendar" as a resource for special days, weeks, or months that can be tied to women's events and activities.

☒ Women's Health Fair. Utilize the expertise of local health-care professionals. Many areas have Baptist Nursing Fellowship, a ministry organization for medical related personnel. Go online to wmu.org/BaptistNursingFellowship

☒ Program ideas: ehow.com

☒ Search online for "Program ideas for women's groups" and you'll be amazed at the treasure-trove of ideas you'll find.

☒ Need new ideas for group projects? Contact community volunteer organizations for ways your group can help women in need. Go to: wmu.com/ministries for additional local, national, and overseas projects.

Ideas for Creating Member or Attendee Bonds

Divide into small buzz-groups if group numbers permit. If not, read out the following sentences for members to complete.

- ☒ As a volunteer, my greatest strength is . . .
- ☒ I'm uncomfortable when . . .
- ☒ I usually try to make people think I'm . . .
- ☒ I love working with people who . . .
- ☒ In this group I have felt . . .
- ☒ I wish I could . . .

Paired sharing—take turns sharing with a partner:

- ☒ Two things you like about yourself
- ☒ One skill you feel you have
- ☒ One of your most satisfying achievements

If possible, divide into smaller groups and ask women to respond:

- ☒ Tell your name, birthplace, and two facts about yourself.
- ☒ Share your favorite humorous story.
- ☒ Tell others what your favorite type of music is.
- ☒ Name your favorite author and tell why.
- ☒ Give one or more reasons why you've joined, or are attending the group.
- ☒ Share about a great vacation you have taken.

SEE THE ELEPHANT?

There's always more that can be said about how a leader needs to use available technology. If you learn how to use it for the benefit of your group, you will not only save energy and time, but you will be less frustrated. Did you think, *Wait a minute! Do I really need to be technologically savvy to lead?* Yes, you do!

As we've already said, tremendous changes have occurred in how women communicate and relate to each other. These technological advances affect the group's basic design. Personally, I was getting used to emailing, and now I've been told this is "so yesterday." My daughter tells me I send text messages like no one she's ever seen! Now that I have embraced more technology, I find myself impatient with anyone whose cell phone can't receive photos.

Are there benefits to all these new ways of communicating? Of course. There's the speed of delivery, better access to information, faster decision-making, improved planning capabilities, and the ability to document communication. My daughter sent a series of messages to parents of her choral students over a period of time, keeping all her communications on her computer. When a parent insisted they hadn't known about a mandatory choral event and that her son missed, my daughter was able to retrieve the messages as proof that multiple notices had been sent. I serve on my church's women's ministries leadership team. Our director is able to not only remind us of deadlines, and so on but to facilitate speedy decision-making without having additional meetings because of her technological skills. These capabilities may mean that meetings may not be as important for your group as they once were. While all of the above are advantages of technology and are usually positive, there are disadvantages also.

Leaders must guard against substituting technology for personal time with their group members. We all are aware of the misunderstandings that can occur when we can't see body language and facial expressions. We can't tell when someone is joking or being sarcastic. Unfortunately when we "read between the lines" in an email or text message, we could be assuming things that weren't intended. It's tempting, because we have the ability to do so, to send too much information to group members and create info overload.

In the past leaders worried about mail reaching members prior to a meeting and waiting for return calls about attendance. The click of a mouse has changed all of that! Speedy responses come almost immediately and multiple revised agendas and information can go back and forth with little effort. The elephant is not perhaps as threatening to group building—if the leader exercises common sense, respect for others' time, and is sensitive to differing expectations.

YOU, THE LEADER

I've read books on leadership, led leadership training, and taught the characteristics of an effective leader, but to me, effective leadership boils down to two basic qualities: *compassion* (agape love) and *encouragement*. People are looking for leaders who will pray for them, and they are looking for a place to belong, to be significant and accepted. Under your leadership, your group can meet these needs.

THE FIVE B'S OF GROUP LEADING

1. Be an Encourager

⫷ ENCOURAGE ⫸

Jesus modeled encouragement for His followers. He changed Simon's name to Peter, which means "rock" (John 1:40–42). He referred to Nathanael as "a true Israelite" (John 1:47–51) and

Zacchaeus as "son of Abraham" (Luke 19:1–10). He forgave the sinful woman who washed His feet with her tears (Luke 7:36–48).

Bringing out the best in others is perhaps the single most important trait of leadership. As the leader of a group, your skills can be enhanced as you learn and practice the principles of encouragement suggested in *The Friendship Factor* by Alan Loy McGinnis.

☒ Have high quality and achievement standards. Communicate these to others.

☒ Be specific when you compliment and encourage others.

☒ Publicly affirm the good things about others.

☒ Reflect on and point out the heroes of our faith—this challenges us to be better followers of Christ.

☒ Be sincere because people will know if you are or not! If they question your motives in this area, they will question them in other areas as well. If you see yourself as an encourager, you are on your way to becoming a successful leader.

2. Be Decisive

As the group leader, the need for decisions comes often and in many forms. Knowing that you will make mistakes must not paralyze you to the point that you make no decisions at all. When wrong decisions are made, analyze the problem and look for a workable solution.

One of our church's major missions events was a "Back-to-School" dinner and clothing distribution for economically disadvantaged children. One year, a major hurdle appeared.

The event had always been held in a space that, at best, would accommodate 250 people. When it became obvious that we were going to attract close to 500 people, people panicked. In my absence as the leader, the group decided, due to tight scheduling issues, to leave the event in the smaller room rather than move it to the fellowship hall that could easily handle 500. The group had acted decisively, but had made what I felt was the wrong decision. I tried to understand why they made such a decision, but reflecting on our goal for this event, I knew that it was not the right decision. When I returned, I met with the group leaders and together we posed and answered a few questions concerning the space issue. We reached a decision and used a member's moving company to transport all the clothing to the fellowship hall before noon. We had a very successful event that was a good model for identifying and overcoming obstacles. The situation became a demonstration of respect for leadership and success through teamwork, while at the same time maintaining a decisive attitude.

3. Be a Delegator

Sharing leadership is not optional—it's mandatory for accomplishing a mission. One way I demonstrate this principle is to take a plate of cookies to a table of five people and offer a cookie to one, two, three, or four individuals, but never all five. Then after walking away, I ask those who didn't get a cookie how they feel. Responses vary from "left out" and "awkward" to "why me?" Once my point has been made, I give cookies to those who were omitted the first time.

Shared leadership will help a group reach its goals, cut the time it takes to reach them, make the journey more fun, distribute the strength it takes to accomplish goals, and help others feel needed and wanted. Scripture offers many examples and patterns of shared leadership: King David and his army, Gideon and 300 hand-picked soldiers, Noah and his sons, who built the ark, and Paul, who worked with and through many Christians.

Failure to delegate limits the leader's capacities. Lack of shared leadership is the number one problem causing burnout in leaders. I've tried "going it alone" on major projects, and yes, I've burned out. However, on projects in which I've empowered others to help carry out the goals and dreams, not only did I not burn out—it seemed that before the project was completed, God was giving me another vision. Putting it another way, "What sound does the band make when there's only a band leader?"

Nancy organized the clothing for the county youth shelter using other volunteers. Becky headed up the annual church mission fair, which was a massive undertaking. Both women exhibited strong leadership skills and relied heavily on others' assistance. You need people like them because they provide a foundation for expansion of your ministry and free up time for coaching or supporting other volunteers.

The publicity drive to promote the women's pregnancy center was a time-consuming job, but Mary was conscientious in her efforts to educate people in the area about all the center offered girls and women with unplanned pregnancies.

Not all situations turn out as positively. Alice accepted responsibility to coordinate displays for the women's fall gathering. She had held the position before and thoroughly enjoyed her work, but her new part-time job meant that she left meetings early, missing fellowship with the other women and the support and appreciation of others. She made it through half the year, then burned out and quit.

Delegating the work involved in any group-related function requires that a leader lets go of some of the workload in order to whittle the task down to a manageable size.

4. Be Visionary

Every leader must have a vision and be able to share it with the group. This sharing is critical to the success of the group. How then do we convey our dreams and goals?

1. **Focus on God's vision.** Lead the group to compose a mission statement short enough for people to remember and specific enough to describe what you are trying to accomplish.
2. **Ask** questions about the group's purpose and missions work.
3. **Ensure** that members can explain the mission statement.
4. **Involve** everyone in creating a plan to carry out group goals.
5. **Acknowledge** publicly the people involved and stress the importance of the ministry when a goal has been achieved.

❧ EVALUATE HOW JESUS LED ❧

Cite a biblical example of how Jesus:
✓ *Was an encourager*
✓ *Was decisive*
✓ *Shared leadership*
✓ *Shared His vision*
✓ *Demonstrated good leadership skills*

5. Be a Skilled Leader

As the leader, you have the responsibility of keeping the group expectations balanced. If the primary function of your group is *doing*, members will expect to make decisions, plan, and serve—but not spend much time on sharing and other relational activities. If *caring or learning* is the primary function of your group, members will expect little business to be conducted but welcome sharing and relationship building time, or time to study.

⊱ JESUS ⊰

Jesus Christ modeled group-leading skills for us as He led His disciples. He equipped them to carry on His mission by guiding them as they traveled together, worked together, and learned together. (See Luke 8:1–4).

Leading a group calls for your best in leadership skills.
> *Discover them.*
>> *Develop them.*
>>> *Improve them.*
>>>> *Use them for His glory.*

YOU WANT ME TO DO WHAT?

JoAnn woke up one sunny morning feeling different. She'd gone to bed thinking about the resignation she was going to write, giving up her leadership position of the group of volunteer workers at the Christian Women's Job Corps® site. She was mystified at why she had been unsuccessful at leading this small group of women. But today, she felt OK with everything. Today she was an accomplished, skilled leader . . . .

Wait! This isn't reality. This is a daydream, a fantasy! You will *not* wake up some morning and find a skilled leader inside your body. It doesn't happen that way. Any woman desiring to be an effective leader must develop some skills in how she directs the purposes and activities of the group. The first step in doing this is understanding different leadership approaches and how they relate to group members.

There are no easy answers to the ins and outs of leadership approaches.

An effective leader will lead with a variety of approaches, depending on the situation. You will be more successful if your leadership approach is a blended one. For example, if you work with a group of energetic volunteers on a community project, you may simply guide the process by checking on details. Leading a women's Bible study will require that you are well prepared and direct discussions from a definite agenda. Stepping forward to lead a missions group might dictate that your approach is a "watch-how-I-do-this-and follow-my-example."

Let's look at four specific areas that challenge most leaders. You will become more effective as a group leader and build a stronger group if you can develop these skills.

ASSESS YOUR STRENGTHS AND WEAKNESSES

Visualize a line that's numbered from 20 to 100, a sliding scale (20 needs a lot of improvement; 100 is a real strength). Place an "x" on the line where you believe you are in the traits listed below.

_____ Enthusiasm

_____ Friendly

_____ Preparedness

_____ Flexibility

_____ Positive attitude

_____ Non-judgmental

_____ Sensitivity to others

_____ Wisdom and discernment

_____ General communication skills

_____ Listening skills

_____ Remember names

_____ Appearance

_____ Organized

_____ Faith

_____ Obedience to God

_____ Dedication

Name your three greatest strengths. List three areas that need improvement.

DEVELOP GOOD COMMUNICATION SKILLS

Leading a group effectively means that you as its leader need to be able to communicate clearly. Facilitation skills are listed below. Next to each write what you could say to encourage members to respond positively. For example:

• Demonstrate listening and invite participation:

  Tell me more . . .

• Encourage reflection: _____

- Getting clarification: _____
- Probing into a situation: _____
  _____
- Confronting member to refocus them: _____
  _____
- Being supportive and affirming: _____
  _____
- Summarizing: _____
- Evaluating: _____

LEARN TO ASK

Learn the art of asking questions: It's important that every group leader develop skill in asking pertinent, probing, and productive questions. The following suggestions may help you increase your ability in this area.

- Don't "tell" when you can "ask."
- Deal with feelings as well as facts.
- Avoid asking "yes" and "no" questions. Rather, ask open-ended ones.
- Try not to use questions with "right" answers. Giving several options makes people think.

BE CREATIVE

Be creative when using technology: Yes, there is still room for creativity in leadership, and it is worth the effort. A leader who approaches projects, meetings, events, or training sessions with creativity will be rewarded with an energized group, one that is motivated to accept challenges. There are four things you should consider as a creative leader:

Being creative is something everyone can do, not an anointed few. Secondly, *useful and new ideas may emerge as you lead your group to "think outside the box."* This doesn't mean, however, that every idea will be practical or acceptable. *Learn to think past "novelty" and encourage your group to be open-minded, yet realistic, and not overly critical.* Finally, *help group members develop their creativity.* As you get to know them, show them how to use their gifts and abilities creatively. For example, someone who is a computer whiz could be challenged to do some creative marketing for the group. Understand as a leader that a group can generate more creativity than you can alone! Brainstorming activities can generate enthusiasm to try new things. Again, that open mind!

HELP ME PRACTICE!

Below are some possible problem scenarios, followed by suggested solutions. Think about a plan of action you might take. Then read the suggested solution that follows at the end of this section. These examples can become guides to help you recognize situations you must deal with, and consider plans of action.

1. A group member begins talking about information that is not on the day's agenda.
2. A group member's behavior disrupts the group meeting.
3. Group members "chase rabbits."
4. Group members have blank looks on their faces and no one speaks or asks questions.

Here are my suggested solutions:

1. **If you did not have a printed agenda, this is the first step to take in dealing with the problem.** As leader you should

model the desired behavior, with organization, commitment to the project, and attention to detail. If you have emphasized the importance of following an agenda from the start, it will be easier to move the discussion back on track.

2. **Meet with the disruptive person before or after the meeting to discuss any personal problems that you may not be aware of.** Discovering the root of the behavior problem is the first step to take before prayerfully confronting the problem. Never try to resolve the issue in a public setting.

3. **Remind members of the original purpose of the group or meeting.** Use well-planned discussion questions to bring the group back to the project at hand.

4. **Perhaps members don't know enough to ask questions.** If this is the case, take time to give background information on a particular ministry, event, mission project, or Bible study, thus facilitating future discussion.

Ministry project opportunity: Christian Women's Job Corps® is a national women's ministry to help women break the cycle of poverty. For more information about getting involved in this tremendous ministry opportunity, call Woman's Missionary Union® national headquarters at 1-800-968-7301. Or visit wmu.com/ministries.

EVALUATE WHAT YOU WOULD DO

What If . . . ?

1. Half the group members are late or miss the meeting?

2. Two group members are carrying on a private conversation during the meeting?

_____

_____

_____

3. Members cannot come to a consensus?

_____

_____

_____

4. You don't have enough time to complete the priority items on your agenda?

_____

_____

_____

Possible Solutions

These are possible solutions to the situations described above.

1. More than half the group members are late or missing?

    Begin on time every time. Without embarrassing the late-comers, review the agreed start and stop times.

2. Two group members are carrying on a private conversation during the meeting?

    Ask one of the talkers a question. If the problem continues, meet with them after you adjourn to address the issue.

3. Members cannot come to a consensus?

    Have all members been able to voice their views? If it is an important decision, ask if group members participated in decision-making in the past. Make a list of the advantages and disadvantages, and lead the group to draw a conclusion.

4. You don't have enough time to complete the priority items on your agenda?

   If you have not been assigning time limits for each agenda item, start now. If appropriate, assign certain items to a subgroup for discussion and reporting at a later time. With group consent, extend your meeting time.

Remember, JoAnn didn't really wake up one morning a skilled leader, and neither will you! Learning to lead is a process, developed through constant prayer, reading, study, and application.

- Devote some time each day to building your leadership skills.
- Ask your church media center director for leadership skills books and do online research.
- Look for other leadership resources at your local Christian bookstore.
- Take advantage of leadership classes offered in your church or community.
- Go to wmu.com for leadership training events and resources.

TIPS FOR EFFECTIVE LEADERS

- Encourage accountability.
- Be prepared at all times.
- Model acceptable speech, behavior, and accountability.
- Create a safe environment for members to share.
- Communicate clearly and frequently.
- Develop good listening skills and restate what you hear to clarify.
- Stay focused on the group's task(s).

- Take control (don't let dominators rule).
- Ask for input as needed.
- Summarize, both verbally and in writing what the group is doing and has decided.

HEALTHY GROUP CHECKUP

Different goals. Different agendas. Different purposes. Different members. Different perspectives. It goes without saying that all groups are different. It should also be obvious that some groups are healthy and some unhealthy. Sadly, often we overlook or ignore that fact. If we are aware that a group is unhealthy, we often are not sure what to do about the situation, or we avoid dealing with it. First, let's define and compare healthy and unhealthy groups, and then let's examine tools for identifying and improving the unhealthy ones.

Members of a healthy group . . .
- ☒ Feel they belong.
- ☒ Enjoy being with one another.
- ☒ Look forward to their times together.
- ☒ Make an effort to attend all meetings.
- ☒ Take pride in "their" group.

I recall one missions event that required a full day of preparation by the group. Members agreed to work in shifts to get everything together. Some young mothers with children had to leave when their shifts were up; however, others worked through to complete the project. One nonmember was so impressed with the teamwork that she pitched in to help. The cohesiveness was obvious to even a casual observer.

How does this happen? *Diagnosis*: The leader encourages

it by including all members in decisions, plans, and activities. If a leader or member dominates the group, members will feel less ownership.

Health Hint: Group unity does *not* mean that there is no conflict.

WHEN THERE IS CONFLICT IN THE GROUP

Conflict is part of any group's life. We know that not all conflict is negative. If you as a leader suppress all conflict, your group will not be healthy. Because of the diversity found in all groups, conflict will arise naturally. My age could cause conflict if I don't agree with a young mother. A professional woman's perspective on women in the workplace might cause tension when she voices her opinion about when to have an event.

Personality differences may cause conflict because talkers want to discuss every detail while other members want to finish! The age of a group may cause conflict. A service group formed in the 1950s may not attract younger women. Worldviews and personal perceptions can impact the type and strength of conflict a group has.

As leader you need to guide the group to focus on the issue at hand, not personalities or opinions some express. Work to develop trust between members and to manage any conflict that arises. Some conflict can only be managed because it cannot be resolved. Here are some ways you can lead the group to manage conflict as it arises. *Be ready because conflict will come!*

☒ Be prepared to handle conflict when it does occur. To be human is to be tempted by self-centeredness, disloyalty, anger, and misunderstandings.

☒ Keep in mind that not all conflict is bad. Disagreements allow people to express their feelings. Being heard by our peers can elevate our self-esteem.

☒ Good conflict is not so difficult to deal with. It's when conflict becomes disruptive and destructive that it becomes difficult. I suggest seven steps for dealing with conflict.

☒ Confront conflict when it is small, before it grows into something larger.

☒ Try to deal with issues involved, not with personalities.

☒ Recognize the feelings and concerns that others have in the situation.

☒ Focus on facts of the situation instead of rumors or opinions.

☒ Maintain a trusting and friendly attitude with all those involved.

☒ Clarify whether one or several issues must be dealt with, and deal with one issue at a time.

☒ Assemble all parties in the conflict at one meeting, and reason with all of them at the same time. Pray prior to the meeting!

Note: *See Chapter 5 for a detailed discussion: Conflict Management.*

RX FOR A HEALTHY GROUP

Healthy groups don't just happen. Some are naturally healthier than others, but like the physical body, a group needs proper nourishment and exercise to maintain its health. As you read these characteristics of healthy groups, you will notice that many are closely related.

✓ *Rx—Proper motivation:* Members participate because their needs are being met, and they are helping meet the needs of the group. Sustained motivation requires that people know what is expected of them, and usually occurs when members have the opportunity to participate in planning and decision making.

✓ *Rx—Wise use of members' gifts:* Forget the myth, "give a person a job and he will become active!" Recognize that a person's spiritual gifts, needs, and desires should conform to God's will for them. Within the healthy group no member is called on to use gifts she does not have.

✓ *Rx—Respect for the individual:* Christian leaders should be people-centered in their approach to the selection and enlistment of group members. People are more important than numbers, methods, or programs.

✓ *Rx—Accountability:* Members of a healthy group feel accountable to one another, and to the group as a whole. This accountability will affect the way members function in the group, and the way they relate to one another.

✓ *Rx—Balance of leader and member involvement:* Members of a healthy group share with the leader in the responsibilities and privileges of group involvement. The leader of a healthy group does not do all the leading but delegates some of the tasks, both the pleasant and not-so-pleasant ones.

✓ *Rx—Communication:* Two-way communication takes place as information is shared. Members aren't left "in the dark," nor do members exclude the leader from the chain of communication.

✓ *Rx—Attitude of teamwork:* Leaders should emphasize teamwork rather than competition as a group incentive.

- ✓ *Rx—Shared goals:* A healthy group is certainly one that is unified in purpose.
- ✓ *Rx—Constructive handling of conflict:* Not all conflict comes in the form of verbal disagreements. Some conflict usually exists as different personalities try to blend, and the way the group deals with these personality conflicts determines group health.

> *"It's your attitude, not your aptitude which determines your altitude."*
>
> — EMILY MORRISON, *LEADERSHIP SKILLS*

EVALUATE YOUR GROUP

Think about a group to which you belong. Draw two columns on a piece of paper. List the healthy and unhealthy characteristics of this group. What plans can you make for making this group healthier?

LEAD, FOLLOW, OR GET OUT OF THE WAY!

> *"Minds are like parachutes. They only function when they are open."*
>
> — SIR JAMES DEWAR

Myth: Some groups are perfect.
Truth: Groups, like people, are not perfect, and never will be. They are made up of imperfect members, and have imperfect leaders. There are common pitfalls in group dynamics that can be avoided, or at least dealt with when they occur.

Myth: A leader is stuck with a group's behavior and can't change it.

Truth: By being aware of potential problems and by learning skills that will help in solving these problems, the leader can guide members to become a healthy, functioning group. The leader sets the tone for most participant behavior.

Myth: The reason for most groups' problems is a lack of vision.

Truth: A fundamental reason for the majority of our problems is ineffective communication, both with one another and with God. We should always be mindful of the instructions of Proverbs 19:21: "Many are the plans in a man's heart, but it is the LORD's purpose that prevails." Prayer is our communication with God; make it a daily part of your leadership preparation.

POTENTIAL PITFALLS

Problems for groups usually appear in four basic areas: 1. problems related to the basics of the meetings of the group; 2. problems with leadership skills; 3. faulty administrative functions; 4. poor participant behaviors.

As you read the list below, after each statement write the number of the problem area that you feel is appropriate for the statement. For example, a group that is too large has the potential of problems in all four areas: there is a problem with the meeting; leadership needs to deal with the problem; administrative actions could relieve the problem; participant behavior is affected.

- Group is too large
- Location of meetings is inconvenient
- Seating arrangement is inappropriate

- Physical setting is too large, cold, or formal
- Meeting is too long
- Meeting frequency is inappropriate
- Leader is inflexible authoritarian
- Members are not encouraged
- Group is unclear about the purpose
- Leader is often unprepared
- Participants are put on the spot
- Tense moments are ignored
- There is a lack of shared leadership
- There is a lack of follow-up
- Leader is not available before and after the meeting
- There is a lack of emphasis on application
- There is a lack of transparency or openness during discussions
- Members do not know one another
- There is a lack of prayer time
- Meetings are often canceled
- Members have childcare problems
- There is no group evaluation
- There is a lack of participant diversity
- Spiritual smugness exists among some members
- Members betray confidences
- The meeting has become a social event
- Members and the leader have repeated tardiness or absenteeism

HOW TO AVOID THESE PITFALLS

Ask yourself, *what could I do differently to solve this problem? How can I lead members to find a workable solution? How can members help me avoid this pitfall?* You have already taken a first step by identifying them. Being aware of problems, or potential ones, gives the leader an edge. Evaluate each situation and each problem.

FINAL WORDS ON LEADING YOUR GROUP

What can you do when the group you are leading turns left when you want it to turn right? As you develop leadership skills, you will feel more confident about redirecting your group to accomplishing its stated purpose. Here are four sets of suggestions for group re-direction:

1. **If your group can't get started** . . . restate meeting objectives. Use small subgroups for discussions and use flip charts or work boards to list ideas or topics. Ask for specific input from a member or invite a resource person to provide and summarize information. If no progress is made, move on to a different topic or use another approach.

2. **If someone dominates group discussion** . . . thank them for their opinion and ask for other points of view. Ask for a group response and poll the group. Don't be surprised if the dominating person isn't particularly interested in others' views!

3. **If your group has lost its energy** . . . check to see how members feel about the topic being discussed and if you need to move on. If more information is needed before making decisions, arrange for another time to present it. A brief break also may help to relieve tension and refresh the group for more discussion. Assigning subgroups or working in pairs may help to revive enthusiasm.

4. **If the group frequently goes off on tangents** . . . call attention to that fact and bring the group back to topic. Asking

one or two members to summarize previous discussions might prove helpful.

EVALUATION: HOW ARE WE DOING?

Often overlooked, the evaluation step may seem to have nothing to do with how you lead a group, the group's purpose, or the characteristics of your group. However, it is the key to eliminating mistakes, improving effectiveness, and reaching goals, and it should be done before, during, and after every activity.

The Why of Evaluation

The goals of an evaluation are:
- ☒ to discover the need for and make changes.
- ☒ to assess the group's progress.
- ☒ to gather facts and information.
- ☒ to assess success of the leadership.
- ☒ to encourage members as they progress toward their goals.
- ☒ to improve the ministries of the group.

The When of Evaluation

When should evaluation take place? It should be an ongoing process, but specific times should be set aside for reporting and updating. Evaluation almost always improves performance, and there are a variety of methods, such as observations, group evaluation activities, and questionnaires. A weekend retreat, with one full day for evaluation and another for brainstorming and planning, is an ideal time to evaluate your group's direction, accomplishments, and purpose.

The How of Evaluation

What should be included in an evaluation? These suggestions will help you develop your own evaluation questions.

- ☒ How clearly defined are the group's goals?
- ☒ Do members and leaders agree on major and minor goals?
- ☒ Do members and leaders agree on the way these goals will be reached?
- ☒ How would you rate the group's support of activities?
- ☒ Do group members have the necessary resources to achieve their purpose?
- ☒ How well do members communicate with one another and with the leader?
- ☒ How would you rate your own leadership of the group?
- ☒ Do members share in the decision-making process?

Just as every member is different, each group is unique. The best evaluation of your group is one that recognizes its uniqueness, describes your specific group's strengths and weaknesses, and determines if it is reaching its goals. Each member should participate in the evaluation, with the understanding that the group shares all observations. The most effective evaluation takes place as the group members interact and share their comments. As the leader, you can help your members work through any fears and objections they have to these types of evaluation.

Some informal evaluation takes place naturally, whether or not you plan it. It may happen when members share their frustrations or grievances after a meeting. Others may express their discontent by not attending group meetings. Only when critical or reflective comments are heard by the whole body can something be done about the issue. On the other hand, some informal evaluation takes place in the positive feedback you get, in the compliments given, or in visible evidences of a healthy group. While informal evaluations aren't completely reliable, they can help you discover areas where you need to do more formal evaluating.

EVALUATIONS

Following are three sample evaluations, one for the group leader, one for the group member, and the third one to assess group activities. You can adapt them to meet your needs. Use them to evaluate an event or group meeting and your participation and preparation.

Leader Feedback

☒ Did everyone attend?

☒ Did relationships get off to a good start and members appear to be bonding?

☒ Did everyone contribute to the discussions?

☒ Did any person seem to monopolize the discussion?

☒ If prayer requests were shared, did you write them down and follow up on them later?

☒ Did the group agree on goals and objectives?

☒ Is the group moving toward its goals?

☒ Did you feel comfortable in your role as leader?

Members' Feedback

Check the statements that describe how you think the group functioned:

_____ All members participated.

_____ Members listened and were open to what others thought.

_____ Members supported one another.

_____ We openly worked out differences of opinion.

_____ Newcomers to the group felt welcome.

_____ We had enough time for agenda items and used the time wisely.

_____ We accomplished our task.

_____ Our group has activities outside our meetings.

_____ We invite others to our group.

Group-Assessment Activities

Emily Morrison, in her book *Leadership Skills*, suggests this activity as a way to clarify group expectations. You might find it useful as you provide evaluative opportunities for your group.

Ahead of time prepare a handout sheet for each group member.

STEP 1: Name some of the things you hope your group accomplishes this year.

• What do you think the group should expect of its members?

• What abilities or services do you think you can give to the group?

STEP 2: Divide your group into pairs and allow time for each to share their answers.

STEP 3: Change partners and repeat Step 2.

STEP 4: Regroup and discuss the responses.

STEP 5: Compile a list of the group's expectations from the responses they've made.

STEP 6: Develop ideas for ways to implement the voiced expectations.

MUST ALL GOOD THINGS COME TO AN END?

This final phase of group life—ending the group—may be the greatest single influence on how people react to future groups, and how leaders develop as well. Successfully completing this phase is key to participants feeling satisfied, involved, and eager to participate again.

During the final phase of the group's life, the leadership should begin to:

- ☒ Lay groundwork for new groups and new leadership.
- ☒ Lead the group in understanding and dealing with termination.
- ☒ Help group members become aware of the psychology of ending a relationship.
- ☒ Help members focus on the accomplishments of the group.
- ☒ Evaluate and praise accomplishments.
- ☒ Complete administrative tasks.

These principles apply to any type of group—a work task force, a church committee, a neighborhood cleanup crew, a Bible-study group, a community support group, or a missions group.

Termination of a group requires skilled leadership. It means moving from a democratic to an authoritative leadership style. The leader must help members deal openly and honestly with the positive, and if appropriate, the negative feelings associated with termination. Remember, all individuals have different personal feelings about the end of any relationship.

10 REASONS WHY GROUPS END

Group leader Neal McBride has identified ten common grounds for group termination:

1. **The stated length of time expires.** This is the ideal reason for disbanding groups that began with a clearly defined time span or purpose for existence.
2. **The task is accomplished.** Once the task is complete, the group has no purpose for continuing.
3. **The group explodes in conflict.** Usually this would occur fairly early in a group's life.
4. **The group has no covenant or common purpose.** Members agree that continuing without a purpose is counterproductive.
5. **A conscious decision is made to terminate and remain friends, for whatever reason.** Schedule conflicts, members moving out of town, the desire to try something new, or reformation of the group are examples.
6. **Ineffective leadership results in the group's ending.** Action- and need-oriented groups are less patient with ineffective leaders than process-oriented ones.
7. **The group divides to form two new groups.** This works well in Bible studies and some other situations.
8. **The group has poor administration.** Poor handling of issues, such as time, place, frequency, and scheduling, can cause members to give up and stop participating.
9. **There is conflict with other programs.** If people are forced to choose between attending a group and participating in something else, this may mean the end of the group's life.
10. **Members are incompatible.** A group may end because interests and needs are too dissimilar or there is simply too great a variance in age and experience.

IF YOUR GROUP DOES END

Since ending a group can be a stressful experience, it should be done carefully. Friendships built in groups can be among the most meaningful many people have, and there are certain things a leader should take into consideration when closing a group.

1. **Don't be reluctant to talk about the end.** Prepare the group for the last meeting before it arrives. Help members to begin to work through the closure process.
2. **Use a flexible last meeting format.** The most important thing during the last meeting is making sure people go their separate ways with the greatest amount of comfort and confidence.
3. **Have fun and encourage one another.** Encourage members to say good things about other group members or share how the group has been helpful for them. Give everyone the chance to share.
4. **Plan for a future reunion.** If feasible, plan a reunion meeting, so everyone can get together again. Let the members know about other opportunities to get involved in groups.
5. **Pray together.** Make sure your group takes advantage of what they have built together by making their last prayer time as special as possible.

THE FUTURE OF GROUPS

We've taken a brief look at groups and their functions. We've seen what makes them healthy and why we have some pretty unhealthy ones. We know that effective, skilled leadership is the answer to group conflict, accomplishing goals, fulfilling purpose, and being meaningful to members.

A current and ongoing discussion is whether working in groups face-to-face will continue to be meaningful (or even necessary) in people's lives. Our previous discussions of how technology has impacted women's lives and how they relate to others illustrate that even the groups to which we belong are changing in their makeup and how they function. Will virtual groups replace groups as we know them?

I saw this possibility several years ago when I spoke in a church and heard a man give his testimony about such a group that had formed in his workplace. He had been faithful in witnessing to his co-workers with seemingly no response. One day he mentioned a Bible study he had taught on Sunday. A co-worker asked him to email his outline and comments and from that request a weekly virtual Bible study group began! The men never met together as a group but still participated in weekly studies.

As leaders we need to think ahead and anticipate what we might be asked to do. If you work in an office, realize that younger generations of employees are more comfortable with new possibilities than you might be. With the demands of busy schedules, most women feel a time crunch and may be attracted to groups that meet only online. Leaders must be intentional in protecting some semblance of interaction if they coordinate a virtual group. Something as simple as sharing photos will help create that personal element. I'm reminded of a recent television commercial where an older woman posted her vacation photos "on her wall"—only the wall is in her living room. She tells her friend sitting on the sofa that if she's not careful, she'll "unfriend" her!

We will have challenges as we deal with the transformations of groups as we know them today. We will still have to communicate clearly and create effective interpersonal relationships. The final question that remains is: are you effective in the group setting as a leader? Are you the kind of member every leader wants in her group? There are many variables in group work—so many, in fact, that one wonders how any group is effective! We know members' backgrounds, age, and experiences all impact the outcome of a group's ability to grow, achieve, and serve.

As we continue to learn to work together toward a common purpose, may we be in agreement with Paul when he talked about the body of Christ:

> *Just as each of us has one body with many members, and these members do not all have the same function, so in Christ we who are many form one body, and each member belongs to all the others.*
>
> —ROMANS 12:4–5

5 CONFLICT-MANAGEMENT ESSENTIALS

By Shirley Schooley

The story of the conflict between the artist Michelangelo and Pope Julius II over the painting of the ceiling of the Sistine Chapel is an absorbing one. The pope and the artist disagreed heatedly over the new design for the ceiling. The conflict became so intense at one point that Michelangelo destroyed what he had painted, ran away, and became a fugitive. However, the final result, the breathtaking ceiling of the Sistine Chapel, is still regarded as Michelangelo's greatest masterpiece. After Michelangelo returned to Rome, one of Julius's military assistants asked Julius why he had given in to Michelangelo in their disagreement. Julius replied, "I planned a ceiling—Michelangelo has planned a miracle." That "miracle" today still leaves people awestruck and silent. Though there was conflict, we have a miracle of art that has, through four centuries, turned human minds to God.

This story serves as illustration that we can use the conflict that is part of all our lives to enrich and enliven rather than destroy. We can use our knowledge of conflict management to help us repair our fragmented families, groups, and organizations. We can accomplish the extraordinary by learning to live together and work together with acceptance and respect for each other and for each other's differences.

This chapter will define conflict and its sources, the types of conflict, how people deal with it, and the leader's role in managing conflict.

CONFLICT IS

We've all heard children engaged in an argument asserting that something *is*, to which the other replies, "Is not!" Conflict is like that in many respects. All too often we simplify what conflict means when it involves more than we realize, in its source and in its management. So, let's look at some statements in an effort to clarify the dimensions of conflict.

Conflict is not simply a struggle over opposing ideas or values or claims to status, power, or resources. Conflict is not people working against each other. What one wants appears to be incompatible with what another wants; what one gets seemingly must come at the expense of the other. The best that can be accomplished is a compromise where each gives up something in order to receive something else.

Because people have incompatible ideas, **conflict is** something likely to happen in many situations. Whether real or imagined, if we believe important differences exist, we assume also that there will be attempts to prevent, obstruct, interfere, injure, or intervene with a desired outcome.

The definition of *conflict* is composed of the following ideas:

1. an assumed incompatibility of ideas or values;
2. a struggle over status, power, or resources;
3. a goal of preventing, obstructing, interfering, injuring, or in some way making it less likely that other persons or groups will accomplish their goals.

Conflict is more often a sign of interdependence, of a need to work together in some way, rather than a sign of competitive, incompatible goals. People with similar interests are often in conflict as they express different views about the best way to do such things as complete tasks, divide work, or distribute the rewards of their joint efforts.

Conflict is not only interpersonal differences. Much of what shapes conflict and starts it in the first place has to do with factors that are beyond the interaction of individual personalities. Some conflict may be caused by the structure of an organization or as a result of the nature of assigned tasks and the natural differences of individuals.

Conflict is not always a destructive and imposing barrier we would be better off without. Wishing we could live without conflicts or avoid discussing them is the real barrier. It is not an evil to be avoided. Conflict is often a painful experience. This is how the argument goes: "Pain is bad. Conflict is painful. Therefore, conflict must be bad also." While conflict may be bad for us, it can also be good, making this statement seem contradictory.

Conflict is not something that always destroys. What *does* destroy are the harmful ways of handling conflicts, resulting in lost confidence and effectiveness. Conflict is sometimes camouflaged, and dissenting views are suppressed so the organization can appear to be perfect. Conflict is seen as unnatural or inappropriate. While we may strive for a perfect organization, one that is free from conflict, it is doomed to failure if we achieve that, because the organization will be an inflexible one, unable to cope with changes. It will lack the capacity for growth and progress. Conflict is beneficial because it can prevent stagnation, stimulate our interest and curiosity, and be the channel through which problems can be aired and solutions found.

DEFINING CONFLICT

What is a workable definition to help us understand the reasons behind conflict and how we as leaders can be effective in managing it? A useful definition for us is that conflict involves *incompatible behaviors*. One person is interfering, disrupting, or in some other way making another person's actions less effective. While this different way of viewing conflict may seem minor, it has real, practical implications.

Here's a possible scenario involving two women, Megan and Ashley. They have been in the same community volunteer group for four years and have clashed several times over plans for a group project. Megan, older than Ashley by about 15 years, believes her way of doing things is the only way. Ashley, while less experienced, has some fresh ideas she would like to see the group add as it raises funds for a youth shelter. Conflict remains right under the surface in the comments they make, and undermines the effectiveness of the group. Their relationship is a good example of how some conflict will never be resolved because neither woman is going to change her position or beliefs on her own. No one addresses the problem so no resolution takes place.

We will use the term *conflict management* in reference to handling or dealing with conflict. This term does not imply that conflict necessarily ought to or can be brought to a swift conclusion. It also does not say that conflict is either good or bad. To suggest that conflict must be resolved quickly denies that it might be good and implies that it would only be bad. A more sensible approach is that conflict has the possibility of being either good or bad for individuals or groups.

Do not let the use of the term conflict management confuse you. The word *management* implies control of the situation, but it is often clear that we cannot control everything. In *The Eight Essential Steps to Conflict Resolution*, author Dudley Weeks acknowledges that much conflict remains unresolved. He asserts that because conflict is an inevitable part of our everyday lives and can do irreparable damage to our relationships, we must work to minimize its effects.

Many organizations, particularly within the church, have norms that discourage most conflict. Norms are the unwritten rules that have sanctions or punishment associated with them. People live by these norms in order to function as members of a group. If someone fails to abide by the group's norms, that person may be punished in some way to bring them in line with the norms.

Sometimes a norm means that strong action will be taken to guarantee that no apparent conflict occurs within the organization. When it does occur, those who cause it must either leave or conform. This norm does exist in many groups, particularly volunteer groups, and can become a serious problem for them.

Neither the view that conflict is undesirable because it disrupts the organization, nor the opposing view that considers conflict essential to the effective functioning of every organization is absolutely accurate. Some conflict disrupts our organizations, while other conflict is beneficial. Discriminating between the two kinds, however, is no simple task.

Using conflict in the best interests of the organization requires a thorough understanding of the conflict and the ability to manage it in a way that will allow us to benefit from its positive aspects. Skillfully managed conflict has a good chance of being functional for the organization, while poorly managed conflict may tear the organization apart.

~ TWO QUESTIONS ~

What does the Bible say about conflict? Interestingly, the Bible does not condemn conflict. It seems to say that conflict is at times inevitable, but it does not have to be a sin. Christians do not have to agree on every issue or subject. Each of us has been created in the image of God. We do not have to make everyone think like us. Properly managed conflict can even strengthen us. We are stretched as we deal with conflict. Sometimes God may reveal what He wants us to be as we are in the midst of conflict.

The Book of Proverbs has a lot to say about how believers are to guard their words and work through conflict as it arises. Look up the following verses in Proverbs and paraphrase some of them to imprint them on your memory.

- *Proverbs 10:19*
- *Proverbs 12:16*
- *Proverbs 15:1*
- *Proverbs 15:18*

- *Proverbs 16:32*
- *Proverbs 18:13*
- *Proverbs 20:3*
- *Proverbs 21:29*
- *Proverbs 26:21*
- *Proverbs 29:11*

Are there any benefits derived from conflict? Whether conflict is bad or good may depend in part on how skillfully it is managed. The belief that conflict must be resolved or controlled is consistent with the view that conflict is inherently bad. Resolution and control are inappropriate reactions for much conflict, and some conflict should even be encouraged and used to help the organization reach its goals.

Too often we have learned inappropriate ways of dealing with conflict and, as a result, have been left frustrated and unprepared to deal with our personal or family conflicts or those in other areas. The problem is not the existence of conflict but the difficulty that people or organizations have in managing conflict constructively. When managed poorly, conflict can become destructive. Properly managed, it can be at the root of personal and social change. Conflict, then, may be seen as a natural occurrence, something to be expected and not to be eliminated or avoided.

BENEFITS

✓ *Benefit*: Controversy is often necessary if people are to feel committed to decisions. When discussion is used to air different opinions and ideas, people are likely to feel satisfied and believe they have benefited from the discussion. They enjoy the excitement, feel stirred by the challenges of the conflict, and become committed to the new agreements or positions. When the position is different from their own, they better understand why the adopted position is superior to their original one.

✓ *Benefit*: People disclose previously hidden information, challenge their own and others' assumptions, dig into issues, and, as a consequence, understand the problem more thoroughly. The diverse opinions that create conflict are needed to help us better solve problems. Note: You as a leader may need to take actions that will ensure that members deal with important issues they may be burying.

✓ *Benefit*: Conflict can become the medium by which problems are recognized and solved.

✓ *Benefit*: Managing conflict can help us build healthy, productive relationships. People realize that others are not as arrogant or as vulnerable as previously assumed and recognize their ability to work together to deal with their differences.

✓ *Benefit*: Conflict brings attention to the existence of a problem that might otherwise be ignored or overlooked. For example, the women's rights and civil rights movements and their resulting conflict brought important problems into the open in American society.

✓ *Benefit*: Conflict can unify a group, causing the members to set aside destructive or counterproductive disagreements while they attend to the new conflict. Conflict, therefore, can be a motivating force for individuals and for groups and can help create group cohesion and commitment.

✓ *Benefit*: Conflict can sharpen the issues of a problem situation. We may not realize what our own needs and purposes are until we have to describe and defend them as a result of some conflict. We find we must study it and learn about it in more depth than we had, and as a result conflict can be educational for all involved.

✓ *Benefit*: The ideas and logic of others can cause us to question whether our original position is as useful and sensible as assumed. We are motivated to search for new information, strengthening our understanding of the situation.

✓ *Benefit*: We are likely to become more open-minded and knowledgeable about the issue and, if appropriate, change our minds. When we have approached the issue from several perspectives and have not stayed rigidly fixed to our original idea, we are more likely to have a decision that is a good one.

✓ *Benefit*: Well-managed conflict can strengthen both our personal and our professional relationships. As we confront, rather than avoid conflict, we add honesty and zest to all of our relationships.

CONFLICT CAN BRING ABOUT:

☒ **Problem awareness.** Discussing frustrations identifies poor quality, injustices, or other barriers to effectiveness.

☒ **Improved solutions.** Debating opposing views forces us to dig into issues, to search for information and insight, and to integrate ideas, creating workable solutions.

☒ **Organizational change.** Conflict often creates changes in procedures, assignments, and structures that are outmoded.

☒ **Personal development.** Confronting conflicts teaches us how our style affects others and reveals the competencies we need to develop.

☒ **Knowledge and creativity.** Elaboration and listening help us retain ideas and understand their implications. We become more creative as we explore alternatives and integrate different points of view.

☒ **Awareness.** Knowing what people are willing to fight about keeps us in touch with each other.

☒ **Self-acceptance.** Expressing frustrations and important feelings helps us accept and value ourselves, in turn building our self-esteem.

☒ **Psychological maturity.** Addressing conflicts encourages us to consider the perspectives of others and become less concerned about our own.

☒ **Morale.** Discussion and problem solving help us release our tensions and stress, making our relationships stronger and more open.

☒ **Challenge and fun.** The stimulation and involvement of conflict can be enjoyable, even a welcome break from monotony. There is excitement, then, in the idea that conflict is not only a natural part of our lives, but also can teach us valuable lessons about ourselves and about others. As we struggle, we learn how to solve problems and reach useful agreements, and our relationships become stronger, more productive, and enjoyable. We begin to be more confident of our ability to deal with conflict in the future. As we learn that conflict can be managed and does not have to destroy, we can face opposing issues and have less need to impose our way on others.

> *"Successfully resolving differences is essential for the preservation and growth of any relationships."*
> — JEANNE SEGAL, *The Language of Emotional Intelligence*

A RECIPE FOR CONFLICT

What are the ingredients of conflict? If we are to accomplish tasks in our organizations or sustain important relationships, we must learn to cope effectively with conflict. Conflict is very much a part of our daily lives.

As leaders, we are responsible for coordinating and integrating the work of many different people. This blending of the energies and personalities of members of our organization, employees of our company, or persons in our family will naturally result in conflict. In well-managed conflict, though, we highlight potential difficulties, encourage new solutions, and ensure the continued commitment and interest of others. Someone has said, "If two people always agree, one of them is unnecessary." Conflict, then, evolves naturally from our relationships and situations, as well as from our personalities. Knowing the source of a conflict may help you to isolate its cause and deal more effectively with it. Therefore, we will look at several ways of categorizing conflict.

Have you ever found a recipe that looked interesting, but when you put all the ingredients together it didn't work? The same could be said about this recipe for handling conflict. While we understand that some types of conflict are beneficial, unbridled conflict hurts families, polarizes communities, divides churches, and fractures the workplace. The ingredients in and of themselves may have some positive parts, but when they are mixed together conflict results, and the "yield" is a tangle of differences that distract, hurt, and even traumatize. Look at the recipe below and consider if the ingredients are present in any situation with which you are dealing now.

1. **Differences (diversity).** We've talked about how diversity in a group enriches and provides fertile ground for learning and growth. The point is not to do away with differences but to utilize them for positive results. Think about the diversity in your life. Are all your children the same? Even that middle one? What if every tree was a palm tree? We wouldn't have pinecones, fresh fruit (other than dates), walnuts, or shade. Wouldn't you miss the decadent smell of the *plumeria* and the beauty of the *jackaranda* in bloom? Differences make our lives interesting, but they can cause conflict.

2. **Needs.** The best relationship is one where both parties' needs are met. When one person's needs are never met, conflict results. When needs are not acknowledged, conflict arises. Women are good at ignoring their own needs in order to make certain everyone else's needs are met. Conflict that comes due to unmet needs must be resolved or managed.

3. **Perception.** While I'm not bothered by _____ , you may be tremendously agitated about it. The way I perceive a situation may be completely different from how you see things. It isn't always a case of "right versus wrong," but rather the perceptions we form. Our backgrounds influence how we view others' actions and how we judge what they say. It's inevitable that conflict will develop as group members, co-workers, family members, and friends express varying perceptions about anything.

4. **Power.** I used to have a beautiful red suit that I wore on special occasions when I wanted to exude a sense of authority. It was my power suit! When an individual uses her power inappropriately, conflict often results. A leader needs to fulfill the responsibilities entrusted to her and

use the power she's been given for the good of the group. Appropriate use of power means that if you are the leader, you will be prepared to lead, care about those under you, and be committed to accomplishing goals.

5. **Value and principles.** When conflict arises over these two ingredients, it can become a serious issue very quickly and moves beyond facts and personalities, which can be ignored. A leader who ignores this type of conflict is very unwise.

6. **Feelings and emotions.** What powder keg ingredients! Even though slights, differing values, and misused power may be imagined, strong feelings and emotions cause conflict to emerge. It is impossible to think about managing conflict without considering emotions because they are such a big part of our makeup. Conflict can escalate very quickly when people speak emotionally. Leaders must diffuse comments made in anger or distress before the conflict burns hotter and brighter.

7. **Internal conflicts.** All of us have inner conflicts that we don't always show to others. But, is that really true? I have known several women whose behavior and speech mystified me at first. As I got to know them, however, I understood what their actions and words really meant. As a leader I learned to minimize the conflict they created and to work with them to help them see why certain things bothered them.

Just as there are many recipes for bread pudding, the possible combinations of the above ingredients are almost unlimited. Some of the ingredients for conflict will be present in every leadership situation you face. How disruptive the conflict will be is largely within your control if you are informed about the issues as they arise. If you know the women you are leading, and are conscientious in helping work through the external manifestations of misunderstandings, perceptions, and even stubbornness, you will usually be able to manage conflict. In an article, "6 Essential Skills for Managing Conflict," written for *Perspectives for Managers* newsletter, George Kohlrieser states, "Fear of conflict can turn leaders, managers, and employees into psychological hostages who are paralyzed and unable to challenge others."

THE "PIECES AND PARTS" OF CONFLICT

There are many terms used to refer to conflict, managing conflict, and conflict resolution. Several are listed below with brief explanations. A leader who is informed is forewarned!

☒ **Constructive conflict:** is a means to an end because it offers individuals and groups a chance to identify and solve problems and can bring positive benefits.

☒ **Destructive conflict:** is not connected to any goal and may undermine what a leader is trying to do as well as damage the group's effectiveness.

☒ **Intensity:** refers to how closely related the conflict is to important values held by members of a group or group purpose.

☒ **Attractiveness of options:** affects how intense the conflict becomes especially if alternatives are attractive to followers and seem important to the organization's progress.

☒ **Number of ideas:** impacts the outcome of conflict because choices must be made. When the choices appear to be equally attractive, the conflict can become intense.

More Terms

When we as leaders face conflict, there are three approaches we can take in dealing with that conflict. Not every conflict situation is the same, but the approaches rarely vary.

1. *Approach* is the conflict situation when the options available are equally attractive, such as choosing between two movies, both of which you want to see.
2. *Avoidance* is the conflict situation when there are both pros and cons. Finding a solution is good but the choice may mean another part of the issue causes additional difficulty. Providing more parking spaces at church is good but the new spaces mean attendees must walk farther.
3. *Avoidance-avoidance* conflict is the situation where the options are negative and equally unattractive.

SOURCES OF CONFLICT

Conflict can be analyzed in terms of whether it is fundamental or superficial, short-term or long-term. For example, we can imagine a conflict that is long lasting or even permanent between two groups in an organization. Such a long-standing conflict, resulting perhaps from a different view of what the goals of the organization should be, will be more difficult to resolve than a minor disagreement concerning methods for meeting an agreed-upon goal.

Sometimes procedures for doing work may be unclear, poorly carried out, or contradictory, thus creating opportunities for conflict. These difficulties can usually be worked out rather easily. The trick is to identify that you have a procedural problem and do something about it. If you are in the midst of conflict, see if procedures are part of the problem.

Conflicts over goals are usually more significant and more difficult to resolve than conflicts concerning practical means to achieve those ends. If people feel their self-esteem is at stake or is threatened, or if they feel in danger of losing face, the conflict may not be easily resolved. Personality clashes, therefore, can sometimes be difficult to resolve. Of course, when conflict occurs in a group, it usually comes from more than one source.

Here is a list of sources of conflict that seem to exist naturally when a group is working on a project. Conflicts typically arise over the following seven points of contention.

1. **Project priorities**: Group members may differ over the proper sequencing of activities and tasks. Has anyone ever questioned your leadership about determining project priorities? What did you do?

2. **Administrative procedures**: How will responsibilities be assigned? What support will be given to the accomplishing of those assignments? As a leader, have you made inappropriate assignments?

3. **Technical opinions**: When the task to be accomplished is not a routine one, opinions may differ widely on the best way to accomplish the task. Name an instance when you disagreed with how a project was carried out.

4. **Staffing and resource allocations**: How will tasks be assigned? For example, one group member may complain that she gets all the "grunt work" while another gets the easier, more visible assignments. Think of a time when you were unhappy because you were given the hardest assignment.

5. **Costs and budgets**: Money almost always becomes a point of contention in any task to be accomplished. If you have built or remodeled a home, been responsible for a church

or community project, or led a task force at work, you have probably faced this type of conflict. How have you as a leader handled conflict over costs and budgets?

6. **Schedules:** Time is another source of tension. A first question for many of us when facing a task, either simple or complex, is "How much time will it take?" How does this kind of conflict affect you as a leader?

7. **Interpersonal and personality clashes:** Conflict often will arise over ego-centered issues like status, power, control, self-esteem, and friendships. Write a brief description of a personality clash that happened and which you had to address as a leader.

WAYS PEOPLE DEAL WITH CONFLICT

People generally use a number of strategies to manage conflict. We can classify these strategies according to their likely outcomes: win-lose, lose-lose, lose-win, and win-win. You could probably compose such a list yourself by recalling your experiences with conflict. Your list might include some of the strategies described here.

WIN-LOSE STRATEGY

When power is used to force the other person to accept a position, each party tries to figure out how to get the upper hand, thereby causing one person to lose. A win-lose outcome occurs when one party in the conflict achieves his or her goal when the other loses. A leader using this style might say, "As leader, I'll settle the issue. We will . . ."

Generally, each side sees the conflict only from its own point of view, rather than from a viewpoint that considers mutual needs. Although this style might be appropriate if the two individuals or groups involved need to continue to work together, eventually the damaging effects of the win-lose orientation will create difficulties. If we win a conflict with a colleague, for example, she may not be willing to be supportive of us in the future when her support may be critical. The conflict is often not really resolved but continues, perhaps below the surface. The win-lose approach is a tempting one when you have more power than the other person.

When quick decisions and actions are vital or when you are absolutely sure you are correct, this style might be the most appropriate one for us to use. You may be aware of information not available to others in the group.

LOSE-LOSE STRATEGY—AVOIDANCE

A lose-lose outcome occurs if, as a result of a conflict-management episode, both parties lose or fail to achieve all or part of their goals. A typical behavior used by a leader choosing this strategy might be: "Let's not talk about that today. I'd rather move on to something else." Often a leader may feel that she may not have the skills and confidence needed to confront conflict successfully. She may believe that avoiding the situation and requiring others to do likewise is the safest option. When we retreat from a conflict situation, we usually satisfy neither our own nor the other person's concern.

We may also be tempted to use this strategy when we know we cannot win, but we hope that by ignoring the problem the other side will also be unable to win. Of course, in this type of situation the conflict usually does not go away, but becomes even more unmanageable.

Recently I attended a meeting where one of the participants asked an important question that needed to be answered. However, it was one with no easy answer and one that would raise many underlying issues. Conflict over the answer was almost assured. The leader's response was: "We have too many items on the agenda to discuss that today!" If it is not answered soon, the organization may soon find itself facing issues that will make its long-term survival difficult. A positive use of the avoiding strategy would be when the leader decides that the time is not right for escalating the conflict or that this problem will resolve itself over time. For example, two individuals in the group may have difficulty working together, but the leader is aware that one of them is moving soon. Intervention may create even more difficulty rather than solve the problem.

Several years ago, I had a good friend and colleague who lived in my neighborhood. She was in the midst of raising teenage children and was dealing with the many conflicts most parents of teenagers experience. I had seen her handle conflict at work and knew she was not one to avoid confrontation. However, she was smart enough to know that immediate confrontation was not always the best strategy.

Therefore, when she found herself in the midst of conflict with one of her children, she would walk around the block several times, often stopping by my house for a few minutes. Then, in a calmer moment, she would go back to cope with the situation. Such a strategy not only improved her mental well-being but her physical well-being as well. Staying away from a conflict situation until tempers have cooled is not avoiding the conflict, but rather is a specific strategy for dealing with it.

LOSE-LOSE STRATEGY—COMPROMISE

In a compromise strategy, each person hopes to gain a little and give a little. In this strategy, nobody wins all; everyone loses something. Members on a community finance committee using this strategy might make a decision such as: "It looks as if Frances would like to give the youth shelter $1,000. Cindy would like to give the Family Program the $1,000. Let's give each $500."

The decision to share the "pie" rather than have the whole thing is often the way we approach many small conflicts we have in our lives. We avoid arguing continually over minor issues by agreeing that our spouse will choose the television show at 7:00 and we will choose at 8:00, or by letting the other driver cut in even when we have the right-of-way. Some things in both our personal lives and our professional lives are simply too insignificant to warrant an investment in conflict.

LOSE-WIN STRATEGY

What we lose in order to accommodate the other side, they win. Accommodating often is an attempt to appease the other side, perhaps because we believe they are too powerful for us to resist. On the other hand, we may not wish to jeopardize our relationship by holding out in a conflict.

We may accommodate the other side if we see some long-range benefit from the gains they might make. If, for example, a customer stays with us as a result of our giving in one time, they may be in a position to become even better customers in the future. In many relationships, however, this strategy results in repressed anger on the part of the one who continually loses, which will eventually affect the quality of the relationship.

WIN-WIN STRATEGY

The win-win strategy emphasizes directing your energies toward confronting and defeating the problem, not the other person. An open exchange of information is encouraged, and those involved try to reach a solution that meets the needs of all concerned.

This is a good strategy to use when future relationships and cooperation are important and compromise is not appropriate. Those taking a win-win approach do not assume that what one side wins the other side must lose. When we use this approach, we are assuming that the conflict results from a problem that both sides, working together, can solve. Problem solvers try to understand the conflict from the other's point of view, searching for solutions that meet everyone's needs.

Although this approach seems to fit our ideas of how Christians might deal with conflict, it is not always possible to use this strategy. In situations where incompatible goals and values are at stake, or if those involved do not have the motivation or the ability to deal with their conflicts, it will not be successful.

DEALING WITH DIFFICULT PEOPLE

"Real change is not without some discomfort. Facing difficult people is tough, but not dealing with them will lead to greater problems in the long run."
— SANDRA CROWE, *Since Strangling Isn't an Option*

Have you had an experience that illustrates that truth? Oftentimes we encounter difficult persons who seemingly involve themselves in conflict because they enjoy it! What about the person who doesn't want to end the conflict? You as the leader have the task of helping that individual manage or resolve the conflict. How? Be sure you are talking about the same issue. Try to deal with any anger that is present. Look at the atmosphere you have created and formulate some questions to help the person focus on issues rather than personalities.

What about the individual who only wants their way? Make sure they understand they are supposed to be partnering to resolve the conflict. Don't allow their behavior to take charge of you. This doesn't mean you have to be as obstinate as they are, however. A leader needs to avoid engaging in a see-saw type of behavior with power moving up and down. This is the time to ask the person if they are truly interested in resolving or managing the issues or if their interest is in getting control and power.

THE LEADER'S ROLE IN CONFLICT MANAGEMENT

I have a good friend who is an administrator for a firm of professionals. One evening at a party we were both attending, someone asked him what he did. He replied, "I herd cats." After the expected laughter had died away, he elaborated on his statement. "Trying to keep that group all going in the same direction is a real challenge. Some days I wonder how we get anything accomplished."

Does that sound familiar to you? The task of a leader, whether as a manager of professionals, a leader of volunteers, or any other leadership role, requires a commitment to stay the course regardless of the frustrations that may come. Never is this so true as when we try to help our group manage conflict constructively. We may often feel like the person who said, "For every problem, there is a solution that is simple, direct, and wrong."

Success in leadership comes not from our ability to manage when things are going well, but from the way we handle adversity and the challenge brought to our leadership skills by conflict. As a leader, it is your responsibility to move members past the conflicts that would tear them apart, toward a unity of spirit as they pursue worthy goals.

Before beginning to help your group manage conflict, be sure you are starting from a basis of absolute integrity. Integrity that comes from self-knowledge, candor, and maturity is a basic ingredient of leadership. Integrity forms the basis for others to trust us. It then must be combined with sensitivity, tact, compassion, diplomacy, and a genuine caring for others. You must come to the arena of conflict with a servant heart. Then, and only then, are you ready to lead others into and through conflict.

THINK ABOUT THIS

Place a check mark next to the statements below that highlight your ability to manage conflict when it arises in your relationships, at work, or in groups you are leading.

1. I try to avoid disagreements by not stating my opinion.
2. I try to meet the needs of people involved when conflict arises.
3. I want to influence others to accept my position.
4. I want to find a solution that works for everyone.

5. I work toward finding middle ground to resolve differences.
6. If my opinion differs from others', I keep mine to myself.
7. I usually go along with the desires of the majority in a conflict situation.
8. I'm usually firm about advocating my side of an issue.
9. In conflict negotiating, I win some and lose some.
10. I enjoy working with others to find solutions to problems that satisfy everyone.
11. I work to avoid disagreements with others.
12. I stick to my position during a conflict.
13. To resolve conflict, I try to blend the ideas of everyone involved.

How you answered will give you an idea of how effective you are in resolving conflict.

We will spend the rest of this chapter discussing how a leader can manage conflict in the workplace, lead with humor, communicate clearly, and how technology can create conflict for the leader.

CONFLICT IN THE WORKPLACE

Conflict in the workplace is unavoidable. The inability to manage conflict could be your downfall as a leader. No putting your head in the sand! As the leader, there are several steps that are key to preventing conflict from escalating. First, acceptable behavior should be defined. People need to know what is expected of them.

This applies to any leadership situation. Volunteers working on a community health awareness event want to know what's expected of them. Members of a women's Bible study need to know what the leader expects from them. Now that we know this list applies to all leadership situations, let's move to the second step leaders can take.

Second, address any conflict head on. An effective leader will anticipate conflict and take steps to prevent it before it even starts. Dealing with it quickly will minimize its severity. Third, understand what others' motivations are. What's in the conflict for them? Are there hidden agendas behind the conflict? Fourth, how important is the issue causing the conflict. Choose your battles. If it's important, keep open communication and work to manage the issue.

The last step that will help you resolve conflict is to realize that conflict can present opportunities to teach, learn, grow and change for the better. All conflict can be harsh and damaging. Your responsibilities in the workplace may demand speedy and effective conflict management. In some instances conflict resolution may come in the form of reprimands or terminations. I have a friend whose job was to manage a large group of civilian employees on a military base. She addressed conflicts involving governmental decisions, employee complaints, and retirement benefits. She remained true to her Christian standards of excellence while displaying compassion and forgiveness.

Managing conflict in the workplace requires strong, committed leadership.

USE OF HUMOR IN CONFLICT MANAGEMENT

If your relationships with those you lead are strong enough, you can assume that joking about some aspects of relational issues is permissible. Using humor about the frustrations of a situation can lighten a tense atmosphere. Research documents that there are many benefits of humor because it helps put things into perspective and relieves depression. Laughter releases the body's endorphins that override anxiety and negativity. Conflict that arises because of stress, grief, anxiety, or challenging circumstances often can be relieved when humor is used appropriately.

A WORD ABOUT COMMUNICATION

If your communication style as a leader is lacking, you are setting yourself up for countless misunderstandings that can lead to conflict. As you strive to be an effective communicator, keep in mind all the principles we discussed in Chapter 1 on communication. Listening is critical for a leader who wants to manage or resolve conflict. Segal, in her book, *The Language of Emotional Intelligence*, says, "Listening is the healing heart of conflict resolution."

A leader intent on managing conflict will focus on individual and group needs as well as provide options to the group. A wise leader will leave the past in the past and look to the future. It serves no purpose to focus on past conflicts. I was a member of a church that had significant conflict in its past. Although more than ten years had passed, church leadership was still allowing the past to continue to rule everything it attempted to do.

Are you sensitive to undertones in your group? Listen for "red flags" in conversation that might alert you to brewing conflict. If you are prepared with feasible options and have answers before the questions are asked, you'll be a leader who faces less conflict. Doing your homework ahead of time will maximize your influence and move your group forward. While I was coordinating a large team of women and reporting to an executive board that determined budget and policies, I worked hard to be aware of undercurrents, possible conflicts, and to have answers prepared ahead of time so we could implement new ideas and programs quickly rather than spending time managing conflict that could have easily arisen.

THAT ELEPHANT IS HERE AGAIN

Can technology actually cause conflict? Or, is it how we use it that causes conflict? The answer is yes and yes. We need to be intentional in our use of technology because all of us have been involved in conflict as a result of its misuse. We take shortcuts that may create confusion and misunderstandings. The abbreviations we use, especially in texting, are either incorrect or compound the confusion. With fewer face-to-face conversations we set ourselves up for misunderstandings and frustration because of the incompleteness of information. Much is missed when we don't hear verbal pauses or word emphases, see raised eyebrows, or know that someone's mouth has widened in surprise.

Several years ago I received a lengthy email from a member of a team I was leading. She had some issues and proceeded to take me to task about them. Her accusing and aggressive message caught me completely by surprise. I was so mystified; I took the email to a co-worker, hoping he could see what I had missed or what I had done wrong. He felt that an unrelated event probably had stirred up some unpleasant memories and that the team member was taking out her frustration on me. I responded to her message, choosing my words very carefully.

When she received my response, she immediately called and apologized for her tone and accusations. She admitted she had been wrong in her approach and caustic in her comments. As we talked, we realized that none of this would have happened had we talked face-to-face. We were able to move past what had come by way of technology. Obviously, in her angst she had hit "Send" before reading what she'd written. We mended our relationship and were able to work together amiably for several more years.

Go through the exercise below and determine if you have unwittingly used technology in poor taste, too quickly, exhibited anger, or taken shortcuts as a leader carrying out your responsibilities.

Look at Leaders and Technology

When has a poorly worded email caused misunderstanding between you (the leader) and others? (Or when you observed it in another leader)

How can text messages cause conflict?

Is it wise to try to manage conflict by way of email? Why not?

Name two situations caused by leaders who took technological shortcuts.

What kind of conflict can group diversity cause in a women's group?

Reminders for Leaders Managing Conflict

Healthy groups develop a norm that goes something like this: If you have a disagreement with another member, tell that person what is bothering you; if you have a disagreement with the group, share your opinions with the group. Norms that discourage direct sharing of differences between members and the group make successful conflict management almost impossible to accomplish.

Leaders discourage direct sharing of differences when they . . .

1. Tell group members they are in danger of losing something and must present a united front.
2. Tell those group members who disagree with others in the group that they are not team players and need to cooperate more.
3. Tell group members, "I know you will do the 'right thing.'"
4. Hold controversial agenda items until the end of the meeting when those in opposition may have left or are tired and ready to leave.

WHAT'S A LEADER TO DO?

When we serve as leader of a group, we need to remind the group that cooperation and conflict are not opposites and the choice is not an either-or situation. People who work together in a trusting relationship have the confidence that others will respond and listen with open minds to their opinions.

✓ *Remind* group members that they can feel free to state and explain their ideas. As the group deals openly with conflict, they repeat and add new information, present additional ideas, and elaborate on their positions. Through this process, better decisions are made and the group learns that it is possible for a group of people to acknowledge their differences and still love one another.

✓ *Remind* the group to define its common goals and find ways of achieving them. This is essential in conflict management. Until members can see what is dividing them, the conflict will remain and may escalate out of control.

✓ *Remind* yourself that the transforming leader helps group members look beyond what divides them to see the common purpose that provides the glue of unity. The leader empowers the group by helping members find a way to do what they have felt helpless to accomplish by themselves.

✓ *Remind* yourself also that the size of the group will affect your ability to manage conflict. The larger the group, the more difficult it is to understand the complexities of any problem. You may find it helpful to divide the group into smaller, more manageable groups, as this will help individuals use common sense, bond with each other, and maintain good relationships as they struggle with various issues.

✓ *Remind* others that learning together provides the support and feedback needed for personal change.

✓ *Remind* yourself that as the group reaches maturity in terms of its ability to deal constructively with conflict, the members may resist depending on you for guidance. At some stages of the group's life, the leader's support for any idea may generate resistance from those who need to prove themselves by challenging you.

> *"Men [and women] are never so likely to settle a question rightly, as when they discuss it freely."*
>
> — Thomas Macaulay

QUESTIONS FOR REFLECTION

Think about your own experience in a recent conflict. Describe how it might have been managed better if people had been able to talk openly about how to manage it.

IS CONFLICT NATURAL IN GROUP LIFE?

Knowing something about typical stages that groups go through can help us realize that much conflict is simply a natural part of people learning to work together. The duration and intensity of these stages will vary from group to group. It helps to know that even when a group starts out working well together, progress is rarely smooth. Although the group generally begins with hope and optimism, boredom, frustration, or impatience may set in as the activities get underway and members realize how much has to be done. Understanding these stages of growth will help you and your group to avoid overreacting to normal conflict.

Stage 1: Forming

When a group is forming, members are "testing the waters" to determine what types of behavior are acceptable. This stage of transition from individual to member status and of testing the leader's guidance may be a difficult time for a leader. When the group is forming, members usually have a mixture of feelings, such as pride in the group and anxiety about the task ahead. During this stage, members define the task, decide how it will be accomplished, and establish ground rules for acceptable behavior.

Lofty, abstract discussions of concepts and issues may cause impatience and questions about their relevance. Problems such as scheduling future meetings, finding a meeting location, and obtaining necessary resources are also part of this stage. Because these distractions get so much of their attention in the beginning, members accomplish little, if anything, that concerns their ultimate goals. This is a perfectly normal, if somewhat frustrating, situation.

Stage 2: Storming

Probably the most difficult stage is storming, when members begin to realize the task is more difficult than they imagined. They are often attempting to redefine the task, trying to agree on organizational objectives and strategy, and determining their degree of commitment to it. They may experience resistance to approaches that are different from what they have experienced in the past. Leaders must be prepared to deal with group members who may argue among themselves and establish unrealistic goals. These pressures mean there is little energy to spend on progressing toward the goals of the organization. Although this stage is difficult, if a group skips this stage, it may not have looked critically or objectively at all the issues.

Stage 3: Norming

Feelings of cohesiveness develop during the norming stage. New group ground rules (norms) are adopted, and cooperative relationships begin to develop. Conflict is reduced. A group will normally experience a new ability to express criticism constructively and express relief that it seems every-thing is going to work out.

The leader needs to foster an interest in finding mutually acceptable solutions and a shared responsibility for the group's activities without unhealthy conflict. As group members begin to work out their differences, they now have more time and energy to spend on the tasks to be done, and some action may occur. Occasionally, a group will not reach this stage, resulting in its disintegration.

Stage 4: Performing

By the fourth stage, members have settled group relationships and expectations. This is the maturity stage for the group as they begin working toward accomplishing their goals. The group's structure, which emerged during the storming stage, now contributes directly to getting things done. At this stage, the leader assists the group to work through problems and become a cohesive unit that gets valuable work done.

LIMPING INTO THE FUTURE

One leadership essential is to become competent in manag-ing both minor and more important conflicts constructively. As we become more effective, we strengthen our relationships with others, improve our sense of individual competence, and gain the ability to reach and lead others.

As a leader, your most important conflict-management skill will be your ability to bring people together and persuade them to engage in the process of learning to deal construc-tively with conflict. Opening up discussion and getting the other person or group committed to talking is the first step, and the most difficult. The idea of talking about conflict may seem strange to you, and may seem even stranger to the one with whom you are in conflict. In fact, he or she may initially mistrust your intentions and require clear evidence that you are committed to finding a better way to manage conflict.

In Margery Williams' wonderful little book, *The Velveteen Rabbit*, the Skin Horse tells Rabbit that "Real isn't how you are made. It's a thing that happens to you. . . . it doesn't happen to people who break easily, or have sharp edges, or who have to be carefully kept." Like Rabbit, we sometimes wish we could become real without uncomfortable things happening to us.

But life isn't like that. We must struggle, confront, and otherwise engage fully in life if we are to become all that God intended us to be. If in that process we are sometimes bruised and hurt, we can find comfort in the knowledge that through-out the ages God's people have often been in conflict, even with God, but have found acceptance from Him.

Author M. Scott Peck retells the Genesis story of Jacob's struggle throughout a long night with a stranger sent from God. After the struggle, the stranger tells Jacob that from that moment on his name would be Israel, because he struggled with God and with men, and prevailed. And, to use Peck's wonderful sentence, "Jacob limped off into the future."

So we must go, sometimes bruised, perhaps limping a bit, into our future, modeling in the midst of our conflict the for-giving, accepting grace of God.

FINAL THOUGHTS

"Finally, Brethren (Sisters), whatever is true, whatever is noble, whatever is right, whatever is pure, whatever is lovely, whatever is admirable—if anything is excellent or praiseworthy—think about such things."

—PHILIPPIANS 4:8

As leaders we must focus on the positive aspects of our responsibilities. There's no doubt that we'll encounter difficulties in our individual leadership journeys. We may fail to communicate clearly or damage important relationships at work, home, at church, or in our communities. When we don't manage our time properly or get embroiled in a conflict, we might feel as if we are lacking the very skills we've discussed in this book. Our struggle to build healthy groups becomes a nightmare of personalities, problems, and imperfections.

I sincerely hope that the new information included in this revision has been both challenging and helpful. As we continue to develop strong leadership skills, knowing we will never "arrive," I hope we will remember Paul's words and "think on such things."

ENGAGE OTHERS

Use this book to your advantage! Consider these ideas to lead others to develop the five leadership essentials presented in the book.

- ☒ Write a review of this book and post it on NewHopeDigital .com
- ☒ Buy copies for friends and co-workers.
- ☒ Lead a group using the five leadership essentials discussed in this book.
- ☒ Discuss the book on your blog or post something you learned on Facebook.
- ☒ Mention the book in your organization's newsletter.
- ☒ Put copies of the book in your company's break room or reception area.
- ☒ Let New Hope Publishers know about other creative ways you use the book.

ADDITIONAL READING

COMMUNICATION

Adubato, Steve. Make the Connection: *Improve Your Communication at Home and at Work*. NY: Barnes & Noble, 2006.

Fleming, Carol A. *It's the Way You Say It*. San Francisco, CA: Berrett-Koehler Publishers, 2012.

Mindell, Phyllis. *How You Say It for Women*. NY: Prentice Hall 2001.

CONFLICT MANAGEMENT

Thompson, Houston. *Conflict Management for Faith Leaders.* Kansas City, MO: Beacon Hill Press, 2014,

Weeks, Dudley. *The Eight Essential Steps to Conflict Resolution.* NY: Putnam's Sons, 1992.

GROUP BUILDING

Levi, Daniel. *Group Dynamics for Teams.* Los Angeles, CA: Sage Publications, 2011.

Mitchell, Joyce. *Teams Work: A No-Nonsense Approach for Achieving More Together.* Birmingham, AL: New Hope Publishers, 2008.

RELATIONSHIPS

Elmer, Duane. *Cross-Cultural Connections: Stepping Out and Fitting in Around the World.* Downers Grove, IL: IVP Academic, 2002.

Lingenfelter, Sherwood. *Leading Cross-Culturally: Covenant Relationships for Effective Christian Leadership.* Grand Rapids, MI: Baker Publishing Group, 2008.

Segal, Jeanne. *The Language of Emotional Intelligence.* NY: McGraw Hill, 2008.

Thomas, Donna. *Faces in the Crowd: Reaching Your International Neighbor for Christ.* Birmingham, AL: New Hope Publishers, 2008.

TIME MANAGEMENT

Felton, Sandra. *Organizing Your Day: Time-Management Techniques that Will Work for You.* Grand Rapids, MI: Revell, 2009.

Lieker, Laurie. *Time Management: The Time Famine.* CreateSpace Independent Publishing Platform, 2012. Available for Kindle.

GENERAL RESOURCES

Clark, Linda. *Awaken the Leader in You: 10 Life Essentials for Women in Leadership.* Birmingham, AL: New Hope Publishers, 2007.

Mitchell, Joyce. *Soul Spa: Spiritual Therapy for Women in Leadership.* Birmingham, AL: New Hope Publishers, 2009.

Schneider, Grant. *She Means Business: 7 New Rules for Marketing to Today's Woman.* NY: Time, Inc., 2005.

Woolfe, Lorin. *Leadership Secrets from the Bible.* NY: Barnes & Noble, 2002.

WEBSITES

Vocabulary-building: merriam-webster.com/word-of-the-day
Leadership assessments and related articles: mindtools.com
Leadership issues: EmergingLeader.com
Leadership courses: store.franklincovey.com

Accessed March 2015